Kennett

The Short, Colorful Life of a California Copper Town and Its Founding Family

Jane B. Schuldberg

STANSBURY
PUBLISHING
Chico Ca

Kennett

The Short Colorful Life
of a California Copper Town
and Its Founding Family

Printed in the United States of America

ISBN 0-9708922-9-2
Library of Congress Control Number: 2005920038

Stansbury Publishing is an imprint of
Heidelberg Graphics, Chico, California 95928-9411
www.HeidelbergGraphics.com

To Rubie, who lived it—
And to Jay, who wished he had.

Contents

Maps

Acknowledgments

For many years a gathering of certain members of my family inevitably brought up the name: Kennett! A flurry of tales followed. Martha, Hennie, and my mother Rubie, all of whom had actually lived in Kennett contributed most of the tales. These conversations were enjoyed by all, but were absorbed by Martha's son, Jay Corson, who even as a young child had a remarkable memory, especially for family history. He became a living reference work for me while I worked on this book. Sadly, he died shortly before this book went into publication (2004). His sister Marjorie Geballe and her husband Ronald Geballe (who was born in Redding, California, nearby Kennett) contributed many stories and a group of family pictures. John Gilman and his sister Cindy Gilman Redburn, grandchildren of Jake (Golinsky) Gilman, also contributed pictures.

The most helpful contributor outside the family was the Shasta Historical Society, Redding, especially the work of Hazel McKim. She found many old files and newspaper clippings and searched tirelessly for more. I am indebted to her and the other Society members who aided me in my early research.

Thanks to Rudy and Margaret Balma and John Balma of Redding, formerly of Kennett, for time, information and pictures. Dr. Grenville H. Gibbs, retired history teacher, located for me the valuable 1905 Free Press Annual. Many libraries and librarians located material. Among them are Bill Jones, Special Collections, Meriam Library, California State University, Chico; The Shasta County Library, Redding; John Gonzales, California State Library, Sacramento; Holly Hurd-Forsyth, California Historical Society, San Francisco; Glenda Pearson, Suzallo Library, the University of Washington, Seattle; Ruth Rafael, archivist, The Judas Magnus Museum, Berkeley; Don Westpaul, photographer, Department of Interior, Sacramento, supplied many photos; Camille Smith, Bureau of Reclamation tracked down and supplied a copy of the only extant photo of the original Golinsky Mine; in the Department of Reclamation Linda Temple located much correspondence regarding the Golinsky Mine and Dallas Gonzales found, among other things, the plat map of Bernhard showing the streets with family names. Also, thanks to Franklin Cibula and Ira Shadwell, attorneys, Redding; Mrs. Georgia Hanson (an early Kennett resident); Daniel R. Elliott, archaeologist; Rhonda Bowers, U.S. Forest Service; Janice and Frank Viscaino, and special mention of Margaret Kardell, whom I met the first day I began research and who stayed encouraging and interested through these many years. Renee Boyd worked on old maps and made them clear for use in the book.

I am indebted to two dear friends who made arrangements for me to use the University of Washington libraries. I thank the late Dr. Morton Kroll and Dr. Gordon Griffith. Also thanks to dear friends Pat Wilson and Joy Hirschstein, who listened to me for years and actually read the manuscript. Gratitude to Phyl Manning for generously sharing her knowledge of book publishing.

My son, David Schuldberg, offered encouragement and read and edited several versions of the manuscript; his faith in the story kept me going. To him, many thanks. My daughter, Jean Schuldberg, typed the first manuscript from my pencil notes and convinced me that I really had a book. She lent much needed support and encouragement. Her husband, Tom Fox, also read early versions and did a wonderful editing of the final draft.

My granddaughters, Nicky and Louise Fox, gave me invaluable assistance in learning to use a computer, and did a great deal of necessary typing for me. Thanks are due to them.

I am grateful to Larry S. Jackson, my publisher, who took over just when I needed him.

Please note, that any errors of fact are due to my interpretation of them. There are many more tales of Kennett buried in Shasta Lake. I hope this book will stimulate others to write about them.

Introduction

Jane Schuldberg's involved and loving portrait of her family's home town was a pleasure to read. Family stories and meticulous primary and secondary research is woven together here, taking it far beyond the normal reminiscences so prevalent in the literature of "places." What's more, the author's sense of place and sense of humor is found everywhere. A very delightful and readable story.

Schuldberg builds the story of Kennett chapter by chapter, following the needed discussion of the broad range of family life with great insight into the influence of early and profuse amounts of mining capital into the Shasta County nineteenth century economy. These large and some small mining operations (the author delves into the confusing history of the myriad of mining operations) provide for expanding populations creating great wealth, but are pitted early on against the equally powerful forces of litigation attempting to stop water and air pollution from taking over of Shasta County agriculture. Consistent with mining and manufacturing of finished goods, the United States copper industry displayed a familiar boom and bust chronology, finally crashing when worldwide use of copper and prices drop after World War I. People and industry depart, leaving the town and surrounding area open to the formation of the federal Central Valley Project and burying of Kennett by the waters of Shasta Lake (1944).

The thirsty desert that is California has come to rely more and more upon the water impounded by Shasta. Schuldberg's afterword sums up the problems of continually mounting use of water for California's southland. In noting the plans to possibly raise the dam by 18.5 feet, polititian Diane Feinstein stated, "I believe it is a God-given right as Californians to be able to water gardens and lawns." The author states "Opponents located above Shasta Dam feel they have a God-given right not to be flooded."

So be it.

William A. Jones
January 11, 2005

Preface

Shasta Lake from the air resembles the arms of a giant octopus with tentacles of various lengths and widths. It is not the usual idea of a lake with its oval or roundish form and somewhat regular shoreline. Viewing Shasta Lake in northern California from the highway, one catches glimpses of some of its twisting tentacles resembling flooded rivers. In fact, this is what they are.

Shasta Lake is made up of the flooded river valleys of three major northern California rivers and their tributaries: the Pit, the McCloud, and the Sacramento. The various arms or tentacles of the lake are known by the names of their flooded rivers. The flooding was caused by the impounding of the waters of these three rivers and their tributaries by the building of the Shasta Dam. Hundreds of feet below the surface of the lake is a graveyard of ghost towns. There lie the remains of the old mining towns of Ydalpom (Copper City), Delamar, Winthrop, Baird, Elmore, Morely, Heroult, and largest of all, Kennett.

Delamar is on the northern Squaw Creek arm and is partly exposed when the lake is low. The other towns are completely drowned. Kennett lies under about 400 feet of water at the deepest part of the lake, about three miles north of Shasta Dam. It should be mentioned here that squaw was once a common name given to geographical features. I have retained these place names, although the word is considered offensive, and many place names in the West are being changed.

Even less known than these relatively recent mining towns are the villages of the original inhabitants of the area, the Wintu (Wintun, Wintoo, Wintoon) Indians. Modern researchers who had a chance to study the area before the completion of the dam (1945) learned from their Indian informants that at least three hundred village sites lie under present day Shasta Lake. What a rich human history lies submerged here!

The dam was built to provide hydroelectric power and to regulate water for irrigation in the great Central Valley of California. Shasta Dam is the second largest and tallest concrete dam in the United States. When the impounded water reaches its full level, the lake formed behind it is thirty-five miles long on its longest arm (the Pit River arm), and it has 370 miles of shoreline. The total surface of its many arms covers an area of forty-six square miles. Viewed from the dam, the lake presents an overwhelming picture of blue water and sky, reddish shoreline, and, to top it off, a view of Mt. Shasta as the backdrop.

The bonus from building the dam was the creation of Shasta Lake, a fabulous recreation area made from the many rivers. For most months of the year Shasta Lake and its shoreline play host to thousands of campers, fishermen, boaters, swimmers, hikers, and sightseers. Most likely few of these visitors know the lake and scenery being enjoyed were created at the expense of human habitation. It is a long timeline from the Wintu villages to the mining towns that replaced them, to the present day lake that covers them.

A chance visit to the dam and a flood of memories started me on this book. During a visit to Shasta Dam in 1989, the Visitors Center had a wall covered with photos of old towns flooded by Shasta Lake. Most of the pictures were of old Kennett. Shocked by this brief look, memories came rushing back to me of tales my mother told when I was a child.

My mother, Rubie (Radzinski) Blumenthal, had spent her teenage years in Kennett living with her great aunt and uncle,

Rosa and Bernhard Golinsky, after her parents died. During my childhood my mother amused me with tales about life in Kennett. Her stories had a Wild West flavor and were full of exciting adventures. Seeing the photos at the Shasta Visitors Center told me in an instant that the site of these tales had really existed. I don't think I disbelieved what my mother told me, but they had a certain air of fable. They seemed so out of tune with the Chicago-area suburb where I first heard them. Living in Kennett seemed so long ago and so far away—so unlikely. The photos now stamped her tales with authenticity. Her stories of life in a Western mining town at the very least were based on a real place.

As I got further into the facts about Kennett, every tale that I remember has been born out by reality. My greatest regret is the realization that I must have forgotten many things I was told, but I am very grateful for those that I remember.

Chapter 1

Going Back in Time

Shasta Lake is located within the present boundaries of Shasta County, California, in the extreme north end of the Sacramento River Valley. Shasta County is said to contain more geologic provinces than any other county in the state of California. It is composed of portions of the Klamath Mountains, parts of the northern Coast Ranges, sections of the southern Cascades (of which Mt. Shasta is the southern-most), the Modoc Plateau, and the Anderson Valley, which is the northern-most extension of the Great Central Valley (Kristophers, 1973). The foothills of the mountains rise abruptly just a few miles north of present-day Redding and climb rapidly to heights of 2,000 feet. Only twelve miles further north 5,000-foot elevations are reached. The Klamath Mountains are steep and rugged and have abundant rainfall. Rainfall in Shasta County varies from fifteen inches in the south to sixty-five inches a year in the north. Most of the rainfall occurs during the fall and winter. Summers are hot and dry.

The Sacramento River, the main drainage system for this area, originates near Mt. Shasta. Numerous small creeks made up of rain and melted snow runoff join the river. The main tributary is the Pit River. The Pit has two major tributaries, the McCloud River and Squaw Creek, which come from the east. There is a second, much smaller Squaw Creek, which enters the Sacramento River from the west just a mile or so above the present day location of the dam and is often confused with the larger Squaw Creek to the north.

Shortly after the Pit joins the Sacramento, the river makes an almost ninety degree turn and flows west for about three miles. Here it is joined by Backbone Creek, where the enlarged river makes another ninety degree turn and resumes its generally southerly direction. The relatively flat area created by the westward flow of the river is a place of great interest. For perhaps hundreds of years it was the site of an Indian village. Then, during the mining frenzy of the 1800s it was known as Backbone, and when the railroad came through in the 1880s, it was named Kennett.

This area through which the river carved its path is known as the Sacramento River canyon and was one of the most scenic areas in a state rich in scenery. The tops of the mountains were covered with deep pine forests and the lower elevations contained many plants and animals, making it suitable for habitation by people. The forests hid deer and elk, and the streams flowed with immense migrations of salmon.

Perhaps for 10,000 years all of California was the home for a people referred to by Euro Americans as "Indians." For the purpose of this book, and out of respect for the natives of the land, the Indians will be called Native Americans. These Native Americans adapted to the specific conditions in each of the many diverse areas of the state. As their populations grew, each group developed its own culture, and tribal boundaries were established. These boundaries were based on the natural features of the land that made sense to the Native Americans.

A specific group of California Native Americans, known as the Wintu, occupied a territory extending from a point about six miles south of Cottonwood Creek to a short distance north of present day LaMoine. On the east a strip of several miles separated the Wintu from the Achumawi or Pit River Indians. The western boundary ran roughly from Hayfork in the south to north of modern-day Trinity Center.

The Wintu people lived a successful life in this area for several thousand years. They used the resources of the land in a skillful manner, feeding and clothing themselves well. They developed family and spiritual structures that provided them with a stable society. While conflicts with their neighbors did occur, in general the Wintu seemed to have worked out, in relatively peaceful terms, any territorial problems.

Within this territory, nine major groups of Wintu have been identified. These included the Nom-ti-pom who occupied the precipitous reaches of the upper Sacramento River, sloping north from the site of Kennett to the north of Delta (DuBois, 1935). However, the greatest concentration of Indian villages was along the McCloud and lower Pit River valleys where the fishing was most abundant and more flat spots suitable for villages existed. It was noted by DuBois (1935) that informants told her that any level ground was used as a village site and soon became covered with huts made of bark. The area called Backbone, later to be called Kennett, was just such an ideal spot. It had a good amount of level ground on a south-facing slope and was near the river.

About 250 Wintu village sites were recalled and identified in later years by one of the last living Wintu elders, Norel-putis. From 1884–1889 he gave detailed information on his people to Jeremiah Curtin from the Smithsonian Institution. Curtin was a fluent linguist and with the help of Norel-putis and his nephew, Mike Reed, they left a stunning written record of the Wintu people. Norel-putis identified the location and names of the villages, the chiefs, the number of houses, and the number of people. In other words he made a census. Curtin considered Norel-putis to be one of the most remarkable people he had ever met. Without their fortunate meeting, very little would have been known of the life of the Wintu. Norel-putis died in 1893 (Guilford-Kardell, 1980).

The only area of Wintu settlement not identified in detail by Norel-putis was called the West Ground or Nom-ti-pom area, which included the site of Kennett. In 1930, another Smithsonian scholar, J. P. Harrington, went over this ground with other, younger informants. Harrington spent a lot of time in the Nom-ti-pom area, and one of his informants positively identified the site of Kennett. Harrington was told its Wintu name, Munuktsiraw or sweet sound (Kardell, 1980), a name possibly derived from noise of the riffles in the Sacramento River at this point. A salmon house made of brush was built over the river here. The shelter allowed the Wintu to spear fish in the river without casting a shadow on the water. Another hint that the river was shallow in the area was the growth of a reed called citapo, which grew here in abundance. This reed was identified for Harrington by a female informant who also told him that this was a willow-like plant that was tough and flexible and was very useful for making the framework on their baskets. This plant was known to grow in relatively shallow water.

In all probability, the first Euro Americans to see this area were fur trappers who came down from the north as early as 1820. Many were Hudson Bay men; some others were French voyageurs. The usual route plan was to work down from the Oregon Territory following the river systems, in this case, the Sacramento River canyon. By 1831, a trapper named Michael LeFramboise had opened a trail in the name of the Hudson's Bay Company. It came to be known as the Sacramento River Trail and, despite its difficult terrain, it developed into the main route south for French and other Canadian trappers.

These difficulties were vividly described in a journal kept by Midshipman Henry Eld on October 8, 1841, as he passed through the canyon. Eld was a member of the George Emmons expedition from the Columbia River to California. The party was following LeFramboise's trail, crisscrossing the Sacramento River sometimes as many as six times during a day's march. He wrote,

"No civilized, sane being would ever recommend the construction of railroads or canals in this region—All the crossings very bad—descents and ascents worse—those of the party who have crossed the Rocky Mountains and the Andes say that the trails are not half so bad as that we have followed today" (Scanlon, 1968).

The first recorded contact of Europeans with the Wintu occurred around 1826 when the expedition of Jedediah Strong Smith and Peter Skene Ogden came into the Sacramento Valley. It seems likely that there had been numerous previous contacts with Euro American trappers or miners, who were now coming into the area in great numbers, but none of these contacts were recorded. However, in 1843, two other travelers did record their experiences.

Overton Johnson and William H. Winter journeyed down from Oregon, and in the winter of 1844 visited the Sacramento River canyon en route to adventures further south. In using this extremely picturesque, but hazardous route, they anticipated the decision by the railroad engineers some thirty years later who chose this same route. Parts of this route were so steep-sided that it is recorded that some of the first miners seeking gold along this way had to build boats and descend by water, trying for gold from their boats. There was not enough flat land to allow them to land (McKim, 1985). In 1848, Johnson and Winter described their journey in a book called *A Route Across the Rocky Mountains.* Winter was smitten with the scenery and described it:

> Having come to the head of the [Sacramento] Valley, we took the west side of the River, which here begins to assume a different character, losing its irregularity and rapidity, and flowing with a more even current. Continuing down the Valley on the West side, we found all along the River, villages of Indians, living in miserable huts made of poles, set on end in a circle on the ground, leaned together, fastened at the top, and covered with grass and dirt. We found those in the upper

> part of the Valley entirely naked, and so wild that they fled from our approach into the thicket, leaving their villages and all their property behind them. They subsist principally upon salmon (which ascend the River in great quantities) upon acorns and wild oats. (McKim, 1985, p. 8)

The description of the Native Americans shows the total lack of understanding on the part of the Euro American intruders. The Native Americans by about 1830 had already begun to suffer a major disaster due to deaths from malaria and other communicable diseases introduced by the fur trappers. The Native Americans had no previous contact with these diseases, and therefore no immunity. By 1835, it is estimated that nearly seventy-five percent of the population had died from diseases. It is no wonder that they appeared shabby to Winter and Johnson. The book by Winter and Johnson was widely read in other parts of the country and was a considerable influence on the number of prospectors streaming over the mountains into California.

California came under United States control in 1846. That same year Commodore John D. Sloat captured the Mexican capital at Monterey and claimed all of California for the United States. Mexico ceded the territory to the U.S. in the Treaty of Guadalupe Hidalgo. California entered the Union in 1850 as a nonslavery state. In 1849, the year before statehood, gold had been found at Sutter's Mill near Colma, and the Gold Rush had begun.

The decade before California statehood had been relatively peaceful for the Backbone area and most of the rest of the northern California. The Backbone area had been but lightly touched by the Spanish/Mexican invasions and settlements. As the Mexicans began to reach territory occupied by the Wintu, conflicts did arise, despite the generally peaceful nature of the Native Americans. According to Heiser (1993) the Native Americans had begun to develop effective fighting tactics and had become adept at self-defense. Heiser (1993) thinks that if the Gold Rush had not occurred, these Native Americans might have driven out their Mexican overlords.

There were but two Mexican land grants in Shasta County. One was made by the then Mexican governor of California, Manuel Micheltorena to Pearson B. Reading. Reading had come into the area in October of 1843, struggling down the Pit River canyon into the Sacramento River canyon using the same trail as the Emmons expedition, on his way to Fort Sutter. Reading become a Mexican citizen and took up residence on his land grant of six square leagues (about twenty-four square miles) running along the west bank of the Sacramento River from Cottonwood Creek to Salt Creek in what is now the city of Redding. The other land grant was made to William Bennitz, who didn't settle his land and eventually sold it off to others.

Reading was the first Euro American settler in Shasta County. Reading was unusual in that he befriended the Native Americans on "his" land. He instructed them in how to work the land and attempted to integrate them into the new society.

Such overwhelming numbers of Euro Americans were arriving that the intruders quickly became the "owners of the land," and the original native peoples became aliens in their own land. The Euro Americans regarded the Native Americans as varmints, just another obstacle on the road to wealth. Any contact with Native Americans was an excuse to kill them. As told in our family, one of the first acts of the Euro American settlers when Shasta County was created was to give a "friendship feast," inviting the Native Americans. The "special of the day" was poisoned food. The first group of Native Americans, realizing the true nature of the feast, tried to warn the others, but failed in their attempt. About one hundred and forty-five Native Americans died from this "act of friendship" (LaPena, p. 324–5, 1978).

After the Mexican War of 1846–47 Reading had a great deal of difficulty keeping his claim. His case was taken to the U.S.

Supreme Court in 1856, where his claim was confirmed. His title to nearly 27,000 acres was signed by President Franklin Pierce and is recorded in the first book of patents of Shasta County.

Shasta County was created in 1850, the same year as California's statehood. The frenzy and lawlessness fueled by the gold seekers had spelled disaster for the Wintu and other California Native Americans. Although California was put under military rule at the time of statehood, events continued to work against the Native Americans. Indeed, some of the earlier military leaders had a brutal tradition of their own. For example, Captain J. C. Fremont's slaughter of one hundred and seventy-five Wintu in 1846 was dubbed by Fremont as an act "to protect the Indians" (McKim, pp. 152, 1985). In 1851, a group of miners burned down a Wintu council meeting house and massacred about three hundred people in the town of Old Shasta. After some negotiations, the Wintu consented to the Cottonwood Treaty, which allotted them thirty-five square miles of land. The Native Americans named Pearson B. Reading as their agent in this affair.

Waldman (1985) relates that "the disruption of their hunting and gathering patterns of subsistence by the rash of mining camps, the outbreak of European diseases among them, and the policies of extermination, with many whites shooting Indians on sight, reduced the population by almost two-thirds within a few short years." Fort Reading was established in 1852 in an effort to bring some form of order to the area. However, it did little to stop the slaughter. The Native Americans, facing starvation, took to stealing livestock, which further incensed the Euro Americans. In 1858–1859, a group of civilians joined by army troops waged the Wintoon War. Several hundred Native Americans were killed, the remainder hunted down or captured and forcibly sent to a reservation on the coast set up to contain any remaining Native Americans. Those that slipped through this net became slaves of the Euro Americans as their only method of survival.

While these Native American wars raged, news of the riches of California spread throughout the rest of the United States and to Europe. Native Americans seldom were mentioned. The main sources of information about miners and gold were to be had in the local California papers, such as the *Shasta Courier*. Items from such local papers were gathered and republished in another paper called the *Daily Alta California,* which was the most useful source of information for would-be miners.

This item from the *Daily Alta California* of June 7, 1852, may be the first published mention of Backbone Creek, and hints at what came to be called the Copper Crescent.

> A party of Germans has recently discovered a very rich gold place on the Sacramento route to Yreka. This discovery was made on a creek emptying into the Sacramento River from the west. This creek is about fifteen miles north of the mountain heights known as the Backbone, and as no name was known for it by the party making the discovery, they called it Backbone Creek. The mining ground is said to be extensive and of unexampled richness. The earth in many places yielded from three to five dollars to the panful. (*DAC,* June 7, 1852)

One of the first Euro American men to settle in the Backbone (Kennett) area was John Sisk, who arrived in June of 1857, having come to the Sacramento Valley from Illinois via the Lassen Trail. He is reported to have said that he had never seen such a beautiful spot as that upon which Kennett stood (McKim, 1985). Some miners were reported to be getting up to $15 a day from placer mining. Many miners hired Native Americans from the small group remaining in the area to do the hard work on their claims. Some of the men, including John Sisk, married Native American women.

Years later in 1909 Elizabeth Gregg gathered information about Kennett (Backbone), and her information about the Native Americans of the Kennett area correlates very well with that obtained by J. P. Harrington and Jeremiah Curtin of the Smithsonian. Gregg apparently did not discover the Wintu name, Munuktsiraw, for Kennett, but she unearthed some new information:

> The Wintu had traditional hunting and fishing camps near the site of Kennett. These were called rancherias by the Mexicans and whites in the Spanish fashion. There was one large rancheria at the site of Kennett, which had a chief named Dowantush. There was another at Squaw Creek (not to be confused with the larger Squaw Creek that is a tributary of the Pit River), and a third one on the east side of the Sacramento at Digger Creek. Each Camp had about 100 people. There were smaller camps all along the river, where there was a flat spot large enough to build a shelter.
>
> The miners hired many Indians to prospect when better relations were established. They would do this job well until paid, going off to spend it and returning when they had no more.
>
> Indian dances were common and white prospectors supplied flour and salmon on these occasions of feasting, even joining in the dancing. The native costume was used at these times, but by 1870, the Indians began to use European style clothing and live in cabins.
>
> Squaws were often taken by white men for wives for $10–15 or a horse in exchange.
>
> Sisk related that one Indian custom was to leave or kill a wife for reasons of bad temper or jealousy. An incident of this type by Tom Dowantush, the chief's son, who killed his wife on Backbone Creek, outraged the whites so much that he was

> arrested and taken to Shasta, tried and sentenced to be hanged. But, Dowantush escaped.
>
> Sheriff Jackson enlisted John Sisk to catch the escapee. To do this Sisk arranged a dance at which he knew Dowantush would appear. Apprehending the Indian there with handcuffs, Sisk took him to Shasta where he was jailed, tried, and sentenced. But Dowantush escaped jail and was pursued by Sheriff Jackson and a Portuguese miner to Squaw Creek where, in battle, Tom Dowantush was killed.
>
> By 1880 the Indians were rapidly dying from disease and starvation, there being few left at the site of Kennett when the railroad arrived in 1883. (McKim, 1985, p. 78)

As Gregg notes, by 1880, the Native Americans had all but disappeared from Shasta County (McKim, 1985). Those who remained were treated as slaves, except possibly the women who had been married to Euro American men. The children of these unions were half-Wintu, and their treatment varied according to the status of their parents (usually the Euro American father) and their own abilities. The general attitude around Backbone and similar communities was to get ahead with life, which meant prosperity and growth in the Euro American community. The native people in the area had become a footnote to history.

Chapter 2

The Coming of the Railroad

As early as 1849, people in northern California and southern Oregon had been trying to establish a north–south railroad line to tie many small isolated settlements together. To grow, even to survive, this string of small communities needed a transportation system to end their isolation and to open up trade. A number of starts had been made, but none had the combination of money and expertise needed to succeed. However, one line starting in Sacramento reached Marysville in April 1864.

This route had been surveyed by Simon G. Elliot, who then continued to survey a continuation of the route through Chico, Red Bluff, the Sacramento River canyon, Yreka, and then over the Siskiyou Mountains to Jacksonville, Oregon. From there, it was hoped that the backers of the railroad in Oregon would bring their line south from Portland to meet at some agreed-upon point near the California-Oregon border.

In 1865, the California backers of this plan formed the California & Oregon Railroad Company (the C&O) to build the proposed line north from Marysville. Oregon, spurred by this development, also formed a company to oversee the building of the railroad within Oregon, and they called their line the Oregon & California Railroad, the O&C.

For its part, the C&O sent Simon G. Elliot to Washington, D.C., to obtain financial support and legal status for its railroad, which was proposed to run from Sacramento to Portland, Oregon. In 1866, Congress designated the C&O as the legal entity to lay track and build this railroad. Congress also authorized a land grant subsidy. This meant that for every mile of track laid, the C&O was granted every alternate section of land abutting the right-of-way (a "checkerboard"), up to twenty alternate sections per mile. In addition, the C&O was granted a 200-foot right-of-way through public lands, with arrangements made dealing with rights-of-way through private lands. Oregon had yet to decide how to continue the railroad building within its state. Their tracks were stalled at Roseburg. The C&O began its operation in 1867, and it worked its way from Marysville to Chico and on north.

In 1869, the transcontinental railroad line was completed. The backers and owners of much of this line and numerous smaller lines in the West were known as the Big Four. These men had been owners of grocery or hardware stores on the East Coast. They met during the Gold Rush and formed a partnership in California. They were Collis Huntington, Leland Stanford, Charles Crocker, and Mark Hopkins. Eventually they controlled a large network of railroad lines that gave them great wealth and political power.

With the relatively small C&O doing so well, it is not surprising that it caught the attention of the Big Four. They took over the C&O and, in 1870, changed its name to the Central Pacific; later changed to Southern Pacific. A totally new town, Redding, was developed on a plot of the last relatively flat land before the start of the Sacramento River canyon.

Engineers and surveyors considered the canyon the only possible route north. But, the possible was also considered impossible due to the rugged topography. The engineers agreed with Midshipman Eld's evaluation made in 1841. Sharp ascents and descents and limited or even nonexistent flat space were as challenging as the Andes and parts of the transcontinental line through the Rocky Mountains. The Central Pacific reached the new town of Redding in 1871, and there it stopped, with Redding remaining the northern terminus for twelve years.

What caused this lengthy delay? Many financial and organizational crises occurred. First, there was a financial panic in 1872–1873 that made investors with capital scarce. Then, the Oregon section remained stalled at Roseburg. The Central Pacific, now the Southern Pacific, was faced with the expensive and challenging route up the Sacramento River canyon. The SP owners needed the assurance of the profitable connection to Portland before beginning to help pay for the expensive route.

The Oregon section regained financial stability and resumed track laying in the early '80s. In response, the Central Pacific/Southern Pacific finally resumed track-laying starting from Redding in April 1883, working towards a junction point with the Oregon line. After twelve years of waiting, the people of Redding responded to the renewed activity with enthusiasm. The saga of track laying and culvert and tunnel building was of intense interest in the Redding area. Progress reports were printed daily in the Redding *Free Press*.

Engineers had been sent ahead of the tracklayers to make plans for the tunnels, culverts, and bridges. By June 6 the track laying crew, under Jack Higgins, reached Middle Creek, three miles north of Redding. Headlines in the Redding *Free Press* proclaimed that the railroad had at last left Redding!

Personalities associated with the construction became folk heroes, mentioned almost daily in the local newspapers. Col. James Scobie, a Civil War veteran, had been appointed chief of culvert construction. Culverts were made to funnel any moving water into safe channels under the tracks, averting the washing out of roadbed. Scobie and the other engineers did such a fine job that the first thirteen miles north of Redding were completed four months after construction began. The first of twelve proposed tunnels was at this point, just below the spot called Backbone. A mile north of Backbone, Backbone Creek enters the Sacramento River, which runs three miles east to west. It makes an almost ninety degree change from its generally north to south flow.

In July 1883, Col. Scobie moved his headquarters to this site. As he called each new headquarters Scobieville, he named this one, Scobieville Number Three. Each Scobieville consisted of a moveable, prefab wooden house that served as a home and office for the colonel. This building was surrounded by wooden-floored tents for the other engineers and overseers. Each settlement became a social as well as working center.

During the first summer of construction, Mrs. Scobie and their daughter joined the camp. According to contemporary reports, there was a great deal of lively talk, singing, and dancing in the evenings around the campfires. Miss Scobie seems to have regarded this railroad camp as the perfect summer resort, and invited friends from the college in Berkeley (soon to be called the University of California) to join her. Horseback riding through the hills was an enjoyable diversion.

In establishing Scobieville Number Three at Backbone, Col. Scobie had unknowingly chosen for his site the former Indian village of Munuktsiraw. This site was well known to generations of the Wintu as a pleasant area with an abundance of salmon and other food sources. By the beginning of August, Col. Scobie left the pleasures of Backbone-Munuktsiraw and moved his next camp to the confluence of the Pit River and the Sacramento River.

Ahead of Col. Scobie's fine camps were the camps of the workmen. Over two thousand men were employed laying track. Several hundred were Euro American, but the majority were Chinese. The Chinese workers did the tunnel digging which was the hardest and most dangerous work. There is no record of the number of Chinese who lost their lives building this railroad, but based on reports and stories about the railroad they probably numbered in the hundreds.

A large group of Chinese workers, brought by a Chinese labor contractor, came through Redding in early April. The railroad activity had its effect in Redding where the business of supplying workers was thriving. This first group of Chinese laborers was sent to Motion Creek, twelve miles north of Redding, and set to work on the digging of Tunnel Number One, while a second group was sent ahead to start Tunnel Number Two, located near the confluence of the Pit and Sacramento rivers.

Tunnel work went relatively fast. By May 1 most of Tunnel Number Two was completed and daylight could be seen through Tunnel Number One. Other crews were employed filling in land for the track laying near these points. Five tunnels were planned from Redding to the first crossing of the Sacramento River, a distance of about twenty-four miles. Tunnel Number Two was eighteen miles from Redding at the Pit River, followed by Tunnel Number Three, Horseshoe; Tunnel Number Four, Peach Orchard, and Tunnel Number Five, Sugar Loaf.

It was anticipated that work trains would be able to reach Tunnel Number Two by fall. By the first week of July all bridges and culverts were finished as far as Squaw Creek, located just two miles below Scobie's Camp Number Three at Backbone. By early August, when Col. Scobie established his next camp near the confluence of the Pit and Sacramento, the bridge across Backbone Creek was started, with completion in December. By October, the graders had passed Backbone and were approaching Tunnel Number Two. Another crew was following, laying track to Tunnel Number One.

During this time of furious activity a work camp existed at Backbone that at one time contained about 3,000 people. The camp was quite unruly and the railroad employed deputies to keep things under control. One of the jobs of the railroad, as soon as track was laid, was to bring supplies up to the work camps.

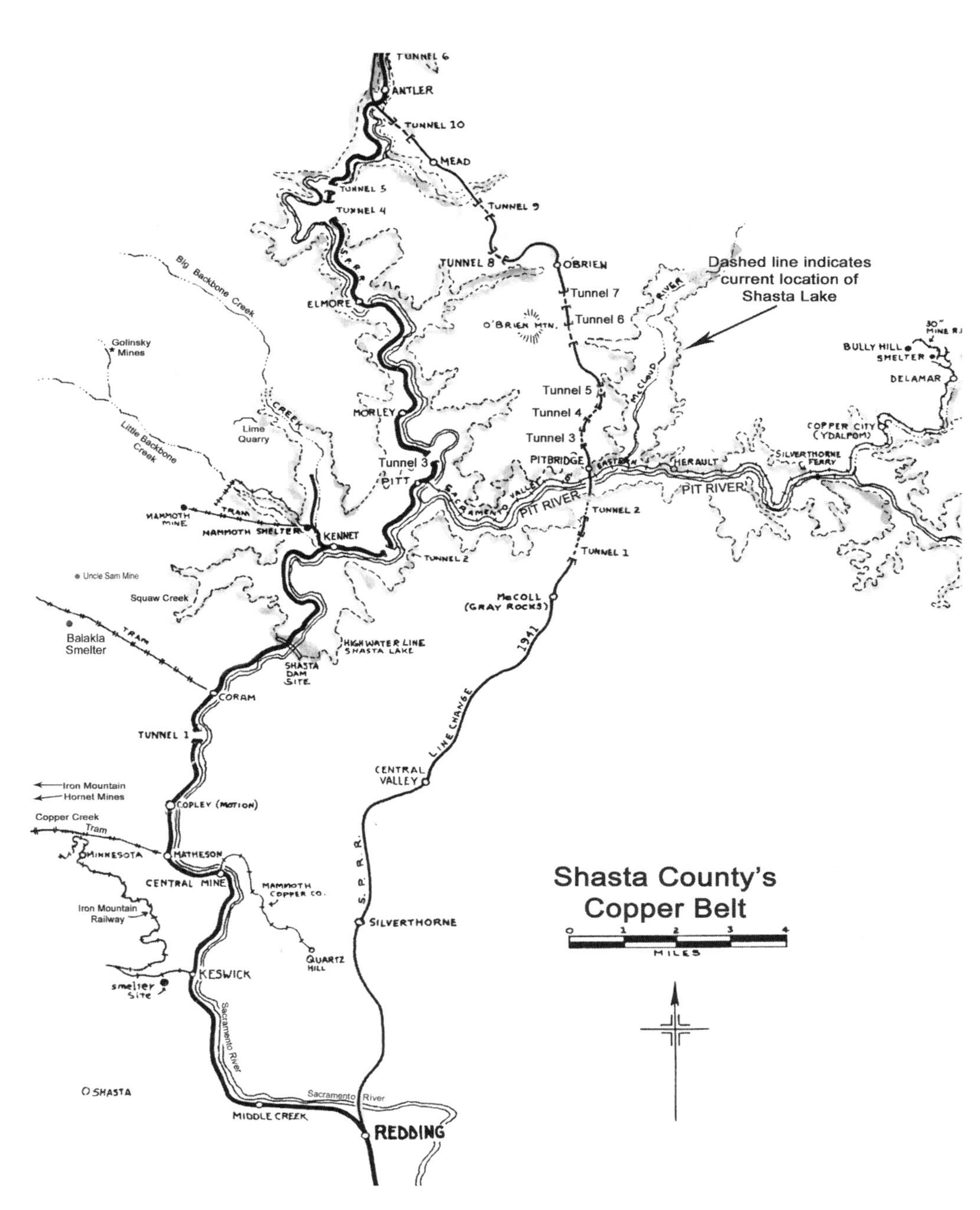

General area of copper belt, railroad routes and extent of proposed Lake Shasta, should a dam be built.

Many small businesses grew up to serve the workers. Variety stores that carried rugged clothing, boots, and tools followed the progress of the rails, and eating places and bars provided services. Many of the tents were occupied by "camp followers."

By October, the road graders had passed Backbone and were nearing Tunnel Number Two. Track was laid, but not through Tunnel Number One. As the fall weather set in, work slowed down. Everyone knew that the completed sections were the easiest on the route; the most difficult part lay ahead. There would be no more relatively flat and straight stretches like the run from Redding to Squaw Creek. The engineers were now employed in building wagon roads to keep supplies moving up the line. Beyond Tunnel Number Two this became extremely difficult as the route now followed the Sacramento River canyon, which was steep sided and narrow. Road and railroad bed literally had to be blasted out of the rocky sides of the canyon.

Even though the main activity moved with Col. Scobie, one of the other engineers kept his camp at Backbone, joined by a group of teamsters. Food was no problem because, in addition to the regular supplies sent up by wagon from Redding, many of the men fished in the river for salmon. The killing of a bear was no unusual event. Fall rains followed by snow in November slowed work considerably. The roadbed was widened with two culverts near Tunnel Number Two, allowing for a double track and switch at Backbone. By November, track had been laid to Backbone and the span across Backbone Creek was nearly finished, to be completed December 3. Then the rest of the railroad crew moved its headquarters and boarding car to Backbone. Construction trains could now run across Backbone Creek, and all was in readiness for the furious activity of spring.

J. W. Malone, reporting for the *Republican Free Press* of Redding (July 28, 1883) sent the following dispatch to the paper:

> A ride today for a few miles ahead of our present scene of operation and somewhat higher in the mountains disclosed to me more fully the formidable and obstinate resistance that our engineers and contractor have to overcome. I thought our present position full of difficulties in the way of getting stores and material transported, but it is nothing to what we may expect further on, where in one place on the other side of the river [Sacramento], a mile of solid rock will have to be blasted out of an almost perpendicular bluff before a wagon road can be made on the line of survey. In some places it is estimated that the cost of grading alone will amount to $80,000 a mile.

Eighteen eighty-four became a year of intense activity for Backbone. Rail traffic through the area kept up a steady pace supplying materials and men to the continuing work up the line. In addition, many significant events occurred in mining. New areas rich in gold were discovered at the idled Mammoth Mine site located above Squaw Creek. Among the new prospectors was Ollie Whitten who also built a store, rooming house, and a saloon at Backbone. Another business established at this time was one of the few to remain when the railroad work moved on. This was a lime kiln built by McIntosh & Ross on land bought from a pioneer settler, George W. Moore, the owner of over 6,000 acres of land.

Chapter 3

Kennett Is Born

Sometime in the fall of 1884, the daily work train from Redding paused momentarily at Backbone, and a young man jumped off the train followed by his small valise thrown by the trainman. Charley Golinsky had arrived at the place newly known as Kennett. The name Kennet had been given to this spot in honor of a railroad man known as "Squire" Kennet (McKim, 1985). Very little else was known about him. He was referred to variously as a railroad man, a financier, a railroad official, but no other details are to be found. In later years, the name appeared as Kennett, with two *t*'s, perhaps through the error of a mapmaker. But this is also the way it is entered in official records, the post office, newspapers, and most local businesses. To avoid confusion it will be spelled with two *t*'s for the rest of the narrative.

When Charley picked up his bag and looked across the track, there was very little to see. There was some evidence of the earlier work camp, as there were felled trees to make flat spots for tents. But the only remaining sign of the new settlers was Ollie Whitten's store. The store would not have thrilled many people, but Charley saw its possibilities as a means to entering the rush to prosperity in northern California. News of the Gold Rush and other tales of wealth had influenced him. He had figured out that the one sure way to prosper was to be the person who supplied the miners with their necessities. The store and rooming house were small, dark, and not too clean. There were cot beds, no indoor plumbing, and oil lamps for illumination. The liveliest part of the whole establishment was the bar, which did a booming business.

Ollie Whitten and Charley Golinsky soon struck a deal for the property. Ollie's mining claims on Squaw Creek now were of the greater interest to him than the store. He had neither the patience nor interest to improve the place. Agreement was easily reached in the fall of 1884. Charley returned to his aunt, uncle, and family in Georgia, and urged them to follow him to the Golden West. He returned to Kennett in the spring of 1885, completed his deal with Ollie Whitten, and settled in.

Charley Golinsky was twenty-four years old, good looking, short and wiry, and energetic. He was lucky to be financed in the new venture by his uncle Bernhard's money. He used it to improve his new purchase. He immediately became popular in the area. In fact, the name Charley was bestowed upon him by the local papers, friends, and neighbors. He had previously been known by his friends and family more formally as Charles.

Charley got to work with great effect. In January of 1886, he was mentioned in the Redding *Free Press* paper as follows:

> At Kennett Mr. Golinsky is doing good business. He keeps a fine stock of goods and what is better still no Chinese truck is found among his wares. The white labor stamp adorns them all. His motto is quick sales and small profits, something that the miner does appreciate. In connection with the store is a good boarding house, where first class meals are served. The present proprietor is evidently determined to please everyone, if there is a possibility of doing so. A boat has been placed up the river for the accommodation of east siders and others, who are taken across free of charge. 'Tis a good idea and will no doubt

> bring him a fair share of patronage. Pack and saddle horses can also be obtained by those requiring such.

The mention of "Chinese stock" in this article is just one small indication of the general resentment and distrust of Chinese laborers. This viewpoint led to the passage of the Chinese Exclusion Act of 1882 and the riots and unrest that followed. A new treaty in 1894 agreed to ten years of exclusion. The male workers were allowed to remain, but no families could be brought in. People were urged to boycott Chinese made goods, hence the approving reference to "white labor stamp," in the item about Charles Golinsky.

The primary elections in August 1886 were held in Golinsky's store. Names in the newspapers about Kennett at this date mentioned as leaders Messrs. Hovey, Williams, Moore, and William C. Ralston. These names continue to be associated with the community of Kennett as it grew.

Kennett was indeed growing. The prosperity of the mines in the area, especially the discovery of gold on Squaw Creek at the Uncle Sam Mine, made it certain that the railroad point nearest the mine would prosper, and that point was Kennett. The Kennett Post Office was established June 18, 1886, in Charley's store and, as Charles Golinsky, he was named the first postmaster. More important than this public recognition was Charley's purchase of the property on which his buildings stood. It had become evident that his deal with Ollie Whitten had been for the buildings only, not the land. Charley purchased this land from the old pioneer G(eorge) W(ashington) Moore on June 16, 1886 (Book Deeds vol. 30, p. 103). By the following year Charley also was appointed the Wells Fargo Company agent in Kennett.

Kennett was becoming a real town. Homes were being built and businesses, such as J. S. Smithson's meat market, began to appear. In the fall of 1888, Charley erected a new hotel that was joined to the old store and rooming house. The new building had six rooms upstairs to accommodate the twenty-four boarders who had strained the space in the old place. These new rooms were like dormitories, except for one, which was taken over by a resident, Charles Butters and wife.

Butters was a mining engineer with his degree from the University of California. He had worked for a number of years in South Africa where he had developed a method of processing ores by chlorination. Butters surveyed the land around Kennett to find a spot suitable for building his own reduction works. He also surveyed a five-mile ditch from Backbone Creek to carry sufficient water to his reduction works. Butters and his wife lived at Golinsky's Kennet Hotel until he built his own house in 1890.

In the meantime, he bought several thousand acres in the outlying area, as well as being busily engaged in buying up a large part of the town site of Kennett. His dream was to create an ideal city out of Kennett. His ore processing plant eventually became a success, making a millionaire out of Mr. Butters, while he continued to invest money in the improvement of Kennett. This was the beginning of a rivalry with the Golinskys that lasted as long as the life of Kennett.

Charley Golinsky continued to prosper as well, though not to the degree of his tenant Mr. Butters. Charley operated a stagecoach to the mines in the area and expanded his stock of wagons and mules for hauling freight. His place became a popular stopover for business travelers as well as those out for pleasure.

In September of 1887 there was talk of damming the Sacramento River for irrigation purposes at or near the confluence with the Pit. To survey this part of the river a group was formed. They hired a logging boat to run them from Bass Ferry on the Pit down to Redding, a trip that combined business with pleasure. The trip of September 3 and 4 of 1887 took two days to reach Kennett by river. Since the group did not travel at night, they boarded with families along the river. Above Kennett was a dangerous rapid, the very place where the previous Native Americans had fished for salmon. The group managed to cross the rapids and reached Kennett for a "good supper, prepared by that genial landlord, Charley Golinsky. ... At Kennett we stayed all night" (*Republican Free Press,* September 4, 1887). This earliest mention of a dam caused not a ripple of interest in the Kennett area, but the idea had been planted—it would grow and not go away.

Work on the railroad connection with Oregon was continuing at this time, and trains were running as far as Delta on a daily basis. On December 16, 1887, the last piece of rail on the line connecting San Francisco to Portland was laid in Ashland, Oregon. There was to be a ceremony with the driving of the last spike to complete the line.

From the time of the first trains north from Redding up to the present, the line had been plagued with all kinds of accidents. This ceremonial day was to be no different. The train from the south was slowed by soft track and bad weather. Two hours were lost at the Siskiyou tunnel while track gangs worked to rerail a derailed construction train. The ceremony was late, but it eventually took place, and the widely publicized Shasta route was open for business.

It was indeed a wondrous engineering triumph. There were sixteen tunnels between Redding and Ashland, eighteen crossings of the Sacramento River, making a climb in elevation from 557 feet at Redding to 3,904 feet at Black Butte Summit and 4,113 feet at Siskiyou Summit in Oregon (Signor, 1982). The line became the principle handler of freight for the entire region and, due to the spectacular scenery along the line, it soon become a favorite route for tourists as well. Even the extraordinary variety and number of accidents at the time seemed not to diminish the enthusiasm for the spectacular train ride.

Chapter 4

The Golinskys Come to Town

January 1888 brought great changes for Kennett, but even greater ones for Charley Golinsky. On January 3 the train brought Charley's aunt and uncle, Bernhard "Ben" Golinsky and his wife, Rosa, along with Charley's sisters, Hennie and Martha, and young brother Jake. This part of the family had been living in Albany, Georgia. A recent fire destroyed their home. Constant urgings by Charley for them to come West finally brought him results.

Henrietta ("Hennie"), Martha, Jake, Charley, Tina, and Ben Jr. were the children of Rosa's sister, Henrietta, who was married to Bernhard's brother, Louis Golinsky. Henrietta and Louis married in Germany and lived in Europe until Louis' death. Then Henrietta brought her children to Chicago. Upon Henrietta's death in Chicago in 1883, Rosa and Ben took four of the children to live with them in Georgia. The oldest child, Ben Jr., had gone to live with an aunt (Rosa's eldest sister Amalia) in New Jersey. Charley moved to Kennett, California. Tina stayed in Georgia when Hennie, Martha, and Jake moved to Kennett with Rosa and Ben.

Rosa and Ben had no children of their own. Henrietta's orphaned brood became an instant family for them. They "adopted" Henrietta, Martha, and Jake; whether legally or only in

Seated, The Golinskys: Bernhard, Rosa, Martha, Hennie, and Jake. *Standing right behind Jake,* Matt Clendenin, mining partner of Berhnard. (Courtesy of Golinsky family)

practice remains a family mystery. In the case of the two youngest—Martha and Jake—Rosa was at least convinced they *were* her children.

When Jake Golinsky had come to Kennett to stay, he was seventeen years old. As mentioned, Rosa and Ben considered him their son, and he is so listed in the *Great Register of Shasta County of 1894,* where it is recorded that Jake's citizenship was granted by "virtue of his father's naturalization." There was some confusion about his age as well, as he is listed as twenty-one years of age. He was a very serious and responsible young man and no doubt gave the impression that he was older than his actual years. Whatever the reason for these discrepancies they followed him to his death, when his son Richard, in giving information for Jake's death certificate, listed Jake's parents as Rosa and Bernhard; not Henrietta and Louis, and his place of birth as Georgia; not Germany. Through all these phases of life, Jake did, indeed, become Rosa's son.

Unfortunately there is no record of what the new arrivals thought about Kennett on first glance. They certainly dug right in to help Charley with the business and build a house for their family just up the hill. Bernhard started buying property in Kennett, and Rosa turned her hand to improving the hotel. I often think of Rosa Golinsky and her life in Kennett. Rosa was a highly educated woman, with an artistic sensibility if not actual talent. She played the piano, sang, wrote songs and poems, and did amateur oil paintings. In the area of crafts she did create some interesting things, namely candles decorated with oil paint that reproduced flowers and butterflies. She also painted trays and mirrors in this manner. I have one of her mirrors over my dresser signed RBG '72. Her first activities at Kennett, as related by family members, were to improve the hotel. She tackled the kitchen and the quality of food improved at once; in fact it became famous throughout the area. Then she undertook to supply good crockery and tablecloths and curtains and rugs. Rosa became a frequent traveler on the train to Redding where she shopped and browsed, mostly at McCormick and Saelzer's store.

Both Rosa and her husband were of German-Jewish descent. They were not religious, but carried on the cultural traditions. They came from a group of German Jews who formed an elite cultural class held together by education and taste, not religion. Many individuals from this group adopted some form of Protestantism. Rosa's brother Carl Jaffe, older by at least ten years and one of the Jaffe family of twelve children, had twelve children of his own. He converted to some form of Protestantism, became a missionary, and later taught religion and philosophy at Heidelberg University.

Because of the liberal attitude of the Golinsky's, they seem to have been accepted readily by the rest of the community. After all, to those around them they seemed hard working, were white, spoke English, and were just folks. Actually, this area of California during the 1880s and '90s was remarkably tolerant in some ways, even to African Americans, who were referred to as colored. A colored wedding in 1889 lists all the guests, both white and black. The list of guests of "both races," notes the wedding presents given by each. While this social acceptance of coloreds is commendable, and quite unusual elsewhere, the Euro American settlers had their hatreds reserved for the poor remaining Native Americans and for the Chinese.

Rosa soon appreciated the climate of her new home and became active in growing flowers and fruits. She is credited with saying: "you put a toothpick in the ground; it grows!" This phrase may not have been original, but she loved to use it. As time went on Rosa become more temperamental, and rather fierce. Some of the children confessed to being somewhat afraid of her.

Rosa's involvement with Kennett had become semi-seasonal. She and Bernhard maintained a small apartment in San Francisco to which Rosa went by herself in order to miss the worst of the winter weather and to keep up her social contacts with various relatives and friends. Thus, the running of the store and hotel periodically fell to Uncle Ben and his two nephews. That this was not enough to keep up the standards they had set for themselves is shown by the frequent ads in the Redding papers for help in the hotel.

If the weather was good, Rosa would extend her stay in Kennett as she did in December 1894. She and Bernhard entertained Miss Esther Schwartz of San Francisco with a musical given in her honor. She would become the bride of a nephew, Emil Golinsky, son of Marcus, one of Bernhard's brothers.

As the "founding mother" of Kennett, Rosa was asked to serve on committees and boards. She declined many but did accept to serve Kennett, along with Mrs. J. S. Smithson, on the board of Lady Directors of Agriculture District #27. The main purpose was to help in the planning for the county fair. She was often heard grumbling about the rain and snow, and expressing ideas for moving the excess elsewhere. She was not alone in her ideas.

One of Rosa's older sisters, Rebecca Jaffe, joined the Kennett

Kennett station and commuter car, 1920s. School children rode it to Redding, as did shoppers. Notice sign spells Kennett with one *t*. (Courtesy of Shasta Historical Society)

community around this time. She was a spinster, a seamstress, and dressmaker. Rosa soon put her to work on the curtains and linens in the expanding hotel. Rebecca, older than Rosa by five years, had already developed some of her sister's proud, acerbic, rigid, and frightening qualities. She was fiercely independent yet had trouble communicating this because of her fractured English. One of her catch phrases illustrating her independence, has come down through the family to this day: "I cook myself and I eat myself!" Rebecca, more inclined to follow family tradition, went into Redding for the Jewish High holidays of Rosh Hashanah, the Jewish New Year, and for Yom Kippur, the Day of Atonement. These services were held in private homes. Rosa would sometimes accompany her but work at the hotel demanded her presence. The men never went, as business was apparently more important to them than religion.

In February 1889, news reached Charley and other busy people in the area that the railroad would erect a depot and siding at Kennett, and that a good wagon road would be built to the mines. The Uncle Sam Mine was pushing new tunnels, other mines were being expanded, and new ones discovered each week.

The family now named its enterprises C. and B. Golinsky, for Charles and Bernhard. In addition to the improvement of the hotel, in their store they added new stocks of miners' supplies and started thinking about building a large new hotel. In May 1889, articles of incorporation of the new Squaw Creek Wagon Road Company were filed with the secretary of state. The road was to run from the Golinsky Hotel to a point on Squaw Creek where the California & Oregon railroad crossed the stream, and then went on to the Uncle Sam Mine, a distance of five miles. Among the members of the board of directors were Charles and Bernhard Golinsky of Kennett, along with L. J. Fader of Redding and S. J. Johns of the Uncle Sam Mine.

The road was finished in the second week of August. Mrs. Fader and her daughter came up from Redding, staying at the

Golinsky Hotel while watching the road being completed. C. and B. Golinsky had a fine team of horses and a stagecoach ready for regular service to the mines. It was noted that "Transportation of passengers and baggage is personally attended to by Mr. C. Golinsky, and everyone who calls here will find him willing to give a helping hand" (*Free Press,* August 31, 1889).

The reopening of the Mammoth Mine also spurred activity in the area. Passenger and freight wagons, called the Golinsky Express, went several times a day to the mine areas. Business at the hotel become so brisk that C. "Charley" Golinsky advertised for help to wait on tables and do housework.

The Old West was still much in evidence despite this modern activity. On August 31, the stagecoach to Weaverville was held up and a Pinkerton agent from Red Bluff was called in to catch the robber. A young man from Kennett was tried in Redding for attempted rape. Progress and crime proceeded hand-in-hand in this latest boomtown, repeating the patterns so familiar across the West.

The winter of 1889–90 was a particularly stormy one. It rained incessantly all of December 1889 with snow in the higher elevations just above Kennett. Tunnel Number One, just below Kennett, had a massive cave-in after a snow shovel attached to a derrick hit the roof of the tunnel. Northbound trains were delayed for a day. The lime house at Kennett fell down, due to wet slopes. In January Kennett had over two feet of snow. Melting snow accompanied by torrential rains caused the wash out of tracks in several places. Many roofs fell in due to the weight of the snow, and there was some loss to citrus trees.

In January and February of 1890, an epic storm raged up and down the route of the Shasta Line. Heavy snow fell for two weeks. By January 4, sixteen feet of snow was reported at Sisson (Shasta). Plows sent to relieve the snowbound trains became mired themselves. On January 15, a train shoved through; it was the last train for forty-eight days. The train out of Redding that same day met heavy snowfall in the Sacramento River canyon.

North of Delta, all three of its engines were stopped by five to ten feet of snow. All 110 passengers, among them Col. Charles Crocker, were marooned and food was rationed. A relief train from Redding was struck by a slide. A snowplow from Dunsmuir with three locomotives became stuck near New Castle Rock. Also stuck were three more engines sent to dig them out.

The ordeal lasted eight days. When the train crept back to Redding on January 23, one hundred miles of the Shasta Line were covered with snow, alternately freezing and thawing. With the rain, slides began occurring all along the line, with a major one at Tunnel Number Two just above Kennett. It was not until March 25 that through service was restored all along the line from San Francisco to Portland.

In the spring of 1890, as soon as the weather cleared, building began again. C. and B. Golinsky, now referred to in the papers as "Kennett's Pioneer Merchants," built a new warehouse and barn. A railroad agent to handle the freight was installed in a railroad car on the Kennett siding. There were stirrings of activity at the old Mammoth Mine. The Uncle Sam Mine continued to prosper, employing over sixty men. Competitors to the Golinsky's hotel developed. A Mrs. Elisa Smith, while waiting for lumber to build a new hotel, put up her guests in tents. In the spring, C. and B. Golinsky improved their popular hotel where, as their ads said, "the traveler can get a splendid meal for twenty-five cents." John Gregg of Holt & Gregg arrived to supervise the building of a new lime house. A meat market was started by the Menzel brothers.

Charles Butters, too, was busy. He kept improving his reduction works and reported to friends that Kennett looked like a small city. Machinery for many mines was piled at the railroad siding. There was great excitement in the whole area as more mines were discovered and old claims were changing hands. Butters' Ore Milling Works was soon doing the assaying for all of Shasta County. His motto was, "one dollar per assay; send by mail or express!" (*Free Press,* October 27, 1888.) Charles Butters' chlorination works now employed ten to twenty men, and received ore shipments from a wide area including Central America. On a quarter section of land next to the Butters Milling Works Butters erected a large, new home. In 1890 he and his wife moved out of the Kennet Hotel that had been their home since arriving in Kennett in 1888.

The year 1890 brought a growth spurt for the whole area, but especially for Kennett. Talk of building trams, of hastening the building of bridges across the Sacramento River as well as Backbone Creek, filled the air. Social life became more active, and during the Christmas season of 1890–91, entertainments were organized and well attended by all. Miss Golinsky sang two charming songs, according to a news report. It did not specify which Miss Golinsky, but it was probably Martha, who was young, beautiful, and alas, fragile. She had but another year to live.

In February of 1891, George W. Moore, the well-known pioneer and owner of thousands of acres of land in the Kennett area, died. With the settling of his estate came a flurry of purchases of his property. Bernhard Golinsky purchased Lot Number Eighteen of the Moore estate for thirty dollars. Other purchasers were Charles Butters, J. S. Smithson, and the Menzel brothers.

By 1890, the Golinsky family and their business interests all centered around Kennett. Charley had begun to branch out and was developing an interest in minerals. It would have been difficult to ignore them with all the potential mineral wealth lying around and with mine claims being filed each week. Charley, however, managed to make a few bad investments and in 1892, he sued to get a $5,000 investment out of the Clipper Mine at Squaw Creek. The case was eventually settled with a compromise. Many signs point to the fact that Charley was getting restless. His wanderings and investigations into new businesses in adjoining counties were routinely reported in local papers. In December of

1892, he bought property near Castella. It was not clear what he had in mind.

It was possible that the arrival in 1890 of Charley's oldest brother, Ben, increased his restlessness. Ben had been living with Rosa's oldest sister Amelia and her husband Phillip Cohen in Paterson, New Jersey. Ben had become a naturalized citizen there in 1882. When these relatives died, Ben left the East and arrived in Kennett on March 26, 1890. He was usually referred to as Ben Jr. to distinguish him from his uncle Bernhard, who also was simply nicknamed Ben. Ben Jr. was the exact opposite of Charley. Where Charley was lively, sociable, and good-looking, Ben Jr. was somewhat dour, a loner, and not too good looking. He was, however, a good worker, clever at business, had intellectual and musical interests, and made himself very useful to the family, managing the large Golinsky store.

While this newest member of the family settled in, another and much more complicated drama began. It begins with the youngest sister, Martha, who was the apple of Rosa's eye. Rosa openly called her "daughter" and doted upon her. Indeed, she was sweet and talented, and very pretty. A group of young men, mostly from San Francisco, courted her. One of her escorts was young Charles Gans, who seemed to have been Rosa's choice for her "daughter." Marriage, however, was not to be; Martha died at the early age of eighteen in the spring of 1892. The notices of her death in the San Francisco papers included a long, flowery, sentimental memoriam signed by three young men. Charles Gans was not one of them. Also included was a long lamentation in verse signed by "Her Mother Mrs. B. Golinsky."

Charles Gans was no doubt fond of Martha, but at the time of her death he was seriously courting Martha's older sister, Henrietta ("Hennie"). Rosa became totally irrational about her loss of Martha and threw Hennie out of the house. Hennie took refuge with Charles Gans' sister in San Francisco, where a year later Charles and Hennie were married. Hennie's brother, Charley

Golinsky, was very angry about Rosa's treatment of his sister. When he attended her wedding, he met Charles Gans' sister Ray, whom he married a year later.

In the meantime, Charles Gans and his bride, Hennie, moved to Modesto. With Charley Golinsky as partner they bought a hotel called the Tynan House. It was described as three stories high and "of great architectural beauty and centrally located" (*Free Press,* December 9, 1893). Charles Gans and Hennie had a daughter, whom they named Martha, for Hennie's deceased sister. Not long after that, Charley Golinsky and Ray had a daughter they named Reta. Thus, a doubly-entwining relationship was established; a brother and a sister Gans married a brother and a sister Golinsky. It seems to be a commonplace with families settling in a new country or a new part of a large country that they end up marrying close relations. Since the opportunities to make wide contacts were small, it seems reasonable that they would form bonds with people within their limited group. All of Charley Golinsky's old friends from Kennett wished him well. Thus, he made his break from Kennett. He had been the pioneer family member there for nearly ten years. The arrival of his older brother, Ben, and then his youngest brother, Jake, and then Rosa's terrible behavior towards his sister Hennie, apparently all added up to reasons for a move.

The involvement of all the young Golinskys in the social life of Kennett is perhaps well illustrated by the report on the wedding of Miss Belle Smith and J. P. Dickinson of Kennett. The list of wedding presents appeared in the paper: a silver mounted mirror from Jake Golinsky, a hair ornament from Mrs. Chas. Gans of Modesto, a silver butter knife and a gold-lined sugar shell from Chas. Golinsky of Modesto.

The Modesto branch of the family lasted for about four years. Charley Golinsky was once again seeking new fields, and in 1889 he moved to San Francisco where he opened an elegantly fitted bar and grill room at 634 Market Street, opposite the Palace

Charles Golinsky, his wife Ray, and their daughter Reta, c. 1890. (Courtesy of Golinsky family)

Hotel. Tragedy struck his sister Hennie and her husband Charles Gans. Charles died of typhoid fever, said to have been contracted during a three-day bicycle trip. He was only twenty-eight years old. The Modesto hotel was let go and Hennie and her child, Martha, stayed for a few months in Kennett with a newly sympathetic Rosa. Then, she and her little Martha went to Macon, Georgia, to stay with another sister, Tina, and her husband. Tina was the only sibling who had not moved to California in 1888.

During 1898 to 1899, events in the outside world penetrated even into Shasta County and influenced the daily routine. The Spanish-American War broke out after the battleship *Maine* was blown up in Havana Harbor on March 25, 1898. The extension of the war to the Philippines, with the naval battle under Commodore Dewey, brought troop activity to West Coast ports. Trainloads of soldiers came down the Shasta route for embarkation in San Francisco. This included a company of volunteers from Redding. The war created some of the events that brought my mother, Rubie Radzinski, from Chicago to Kennett.

My mother arrived in Kennett in March of 1899. She was fourteen years old and had come from Chicago by herself on the train. She was the youngest of four children, all orphaned by the sudden and premature death from influenza of their mother and father in San Antonio, Texas, where ironically they had gone for their health. They died a few weeks apart in 1895 and the children were taken care of by various branches of the family. My mother was taken in by her father's brother, Isaac Radzinski and his wife, Henrietta, who had seven children and a household my mother described as chaotic.

It was a feat of great cleverness for my mother to get herself out of this situation and be sent to her great-aunt Rosa, in

Front row: Bernhard, Little Martha (Hennie's child), and Rosa. *Behind:* Hennie and Rubie. Rubie arrives in Kennett and is adopted by Rosa and Bernhard, c. 1899. (Courtesy of Golinsky family)

Kennett, California. It seems that a rumor was floated that Rubie had tuberculosis, and she was sent west for her health. She did not, in fact, have TB, but was in a very sad state psychologically due to grief over her parents' death, separation from her siblings, and life in the constant uproar in the Isaac Radzinski household. It is no wonder that she helped to engineer an escape to Kennett.

Rubie's brother, Arthur, who was five years older, also managed to elude family plans for him. After his parent's death, he stayed on in San Antonio. He had wanted to become a lawyer, but the Spanish-American War altered his plans and he became a volunteer in the Texas 33 Infantry. Despite the urging of his officer, Major Logan, to become his clerk in Washington, D.C., Arthur became a soldier. He arranged to write dispatches for the San Antonio *Daily Express*.

On October 1, 1899, Arthur and 1,700 fellow soldiers embarked from San Francisco on the USS *Sheridan.* Among the throngs waving good-bye was his sister, Rubie, who, along with her cousin Hennie Gans, came down from Kennett to see him off. A month later, on November 11, 1899, Arthur was killed at the Battle of San Jacinto. Two of his dispatches were published in the San Antonio *Daily Express,* the only two he lived to write.

The news of his death did not reach Rubie for several months in Kennett. In March she received a long, handwritten sympathy letter written by Arthur's sergeant, Herbert B. Harpold, of Company G, Thirty-third Infantry, U.S. Volunteers, Manila, Philippines. A detailed and sympathetic article based on this letter appeared in the Redding *Free Press,* March 30, 1900.

In this interval between Arthur's departure and the news of his death, Rubie came to know and love Uncle Ben and Aunt Rosa and she reveled in life in Kennett and the countryside. These were halcyon days for her, and they formed the basis of the recollections that she told me many years later. As she relived these days in which Kennett became a part of her psyche, her telling made them a part of mine as well.

Chapter 5

Kennett Becomes a Real Little City

Throughout Western America, wherever a railroad placed its tracks, a line of demarcation was created between the rich and poor, the educated and unlettered. The "wrong side of the tracks" is an American idiom. This function of creating an above-the-tracks and below-the-tracks area was determined by the placement of the tracks, but in Kennett the railroad line performed an additional function. Its length became the main street of the town.

Due to the hilly topography and the scarcity of flat land, the railroad had taken over the narrow strip of level land to lay its right of way. In doing so, it created Kennett, a new place for human habitation, that is, for Euro Americans. When the railroad took over the only flat land, its track and a hundred feet on either side formed the main street of the town. This was sometimes called Railroad Avenue and sometimes Main Street. The question of the actual width of the right-of-way led to many lawsuits and countersuits between the railroad and the businesses that were established along side of it.

In addition to creating a double-purpose main street, the train itself became a presence and a new dimension to life. It brought bustle and excitement just by coming and going right down the center of town. It also became a vehicle for sudden death, some-

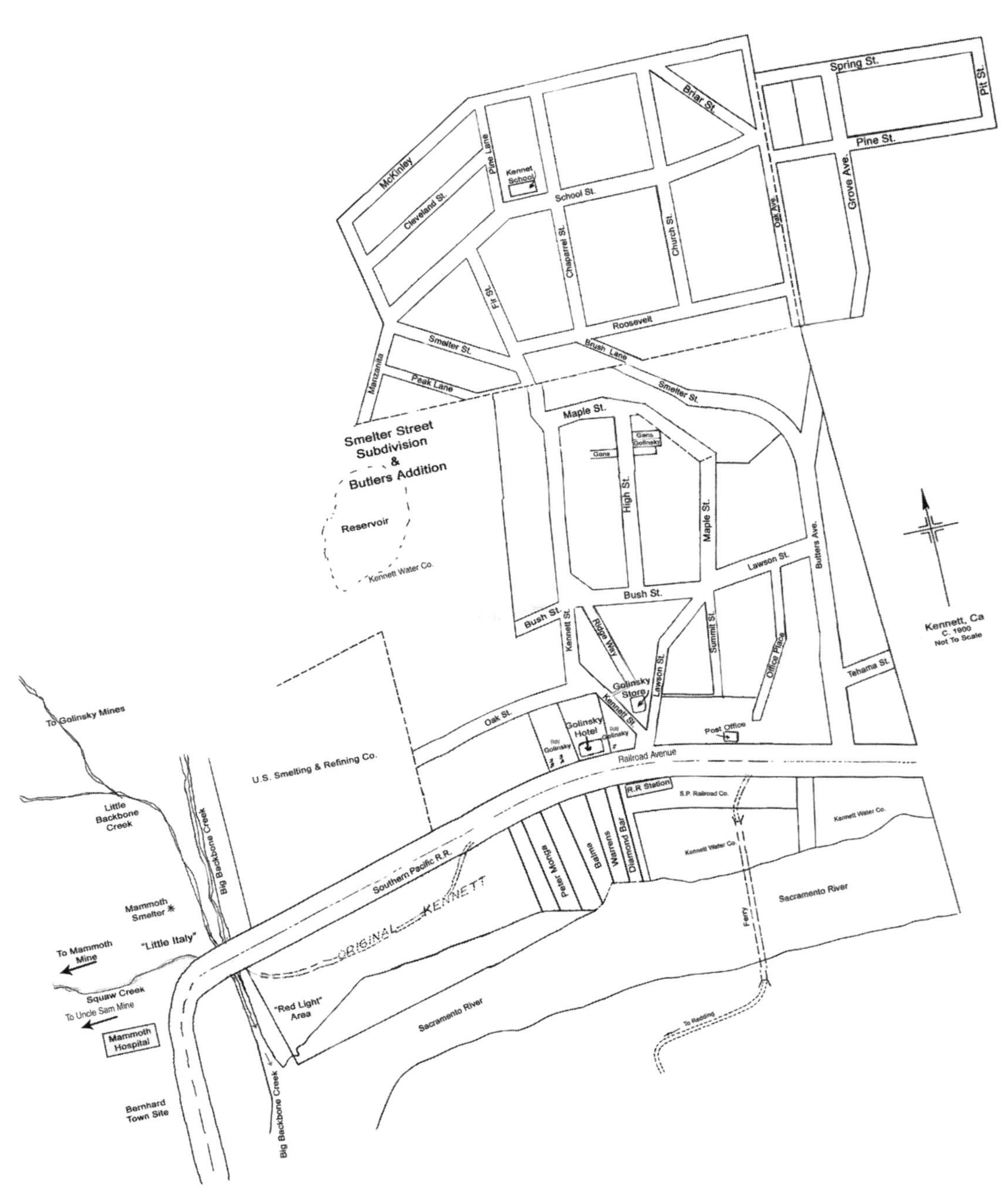

Street map of Kennett. Not to scale. All streets not shown for clarity.

times inadvertent, sometimes intentional. For many, it was an elusive source of dreams about adventure and far away destinations, and a possible escape route to other places, other lives. No matter what, it could not be ignored. The patterns of daily life in Kennett were altered and sometimes determined by its presence. Naturally, the train brought most of the visitors to Kennett and transported local people to other places in the area, or it formed the first segment of a longer trip. In local parlance, "going down" was understood by all as "going to San Francisco."

When my mother arrived in Kennett in the spring of 1899, the railroad tracks and the general pattern of settlement in Kennett were in place. On the north or upper side of the tracks a hill rose steadily and fairly steeply. The first businesses and residences established on this side, including the Golinsky (Kennett) Hotel, were built on lots that had to be partially carved out of the hillside. Just opposite the railroad station, which was located on the south side of the tracks, Lawson Street took off at a right angle from the tracks, pushing up the hill but soon adjusting itself to a more northeasterly direction to modify its steep rise.

Lawson Street and Railroad Avenue become the locations of Kennett's early businesses. On the northwest corner, the first business, Ollie Whitten's–Charley Golinsky's store and rooming house, had been located. The original rooming house had expanded into a two-story hotel that within a few years became a very large establishment. Also located here were Smithson's Meat Market, the post office, and Trinity Copper Company offices.

The south side of Railroad Avenue had but a few hundred feet of flat land before plunging down the hill to the Sacramento River. Buildings on this side, therefore, were started on the small section of level ground and then built down the hillside toward the river. Stilts were used to stabilize the one or two stories that ran down the hillside. On this side of the street the Southern Pacific Railroad station and freight offices were located. Also here were Victor Warrens' Diamond Bar, Peter Monga's general store, and the Balma family's City Hotel which had sleeping rooms, a restaurant, and an excellent wine cellar. They were almost exactly across from the Golinsky Hotel, soon to be officially called the Kennet Hotel and Bar.

As this street extended west towards Backbone Creek, quite a few upstanding citizens built their homes, and restaurants and bars opened up in great profusion. But, about a mile west of Lawson Street, near the point where the river and the tracks turn south, the street became the town's red-light district.

At the time Charles Butters was creating his idea of a dream city, many families, including the Golinskys, continued to enlarge and improve their own holdings. Several family members, including Bernhard's nephew, Ben Jr., and his niece, Hennie Gans, had bought city lots in what was called the Butters Subdivision, located just two blocks above Railroad Avenue. The rest of the Golinsky's property centered around the original town site along Railroad Avenue and crept up Lawson Street. Their newest projects now included the town site of Bernhard, across Big Backbone Creek and near the smelter. And, much of Golinsky's interests were in mining property.

It is historical fact that the Golinsky family had been well established in Kennett when Charles Butters first arrived. In fact, as mentioned earlier, Charles Butters and his wife lived for many years at the old Kennet Hotel until he built his home in 1890. The Redding *Free Press Annual* of 1905 contained several articles about the Golinskys. There it was told of the long residence of Bernhard and family; the hotel and stores are mentioned glowingly, and the new Bernhard town site is boosted. Rosa is complimented on the famously successful "Bernhard" picnic. The writer concluded by calling Bernhard Golinsky "the Father of Kennett" (*Free Press Annual,* 1905).

Whether there was actually a Golinsky-Butters rivalry, this small item seems to point to its existence. In February 1905 at a meeting to organize a band, some "… pretty warm debating was done. Some of the boys said Bernhard Golinsky was to furnish the uniforms and the band was to be called the Golinsky Band, while others said Charles Butters was to do the same and the band was to be called the Butters Brass Band. Still others said it should be called the Kennett Brass Band," (*Free Press,* February 18, 1905) which was the eventual outcome of the debate.

Kennett now had a good marching band, and a somewhat unsteady symphony. The band participated in the 1905 Fourth of July parade in Redding. Kennett had by 1900 two quite good hotels. The Smithsons built a new structure in the spring of 1900 and the Golinsky Kennet Hotel was already enlarged at that time. There were a number of smaller hotels, among them the Balma's, and many rooming houses, as well as rooms to rent from private families. The occupancy rate at the hotels was high, so high, in fact, that roomers frequently had to double or triple up.

Life at the Kennet Hotel was very hectic. Bernhard contacted his nephew Charley in San Francisco to find some cooks for him. He hired two women. Charley advanced their railroad fare, and the women agreed to repay the money from their first month's wages. They arrived on the morning train from San Francisco, but that night they secretly left, taking their baggage through the window of their room. Their flight was noticed by Rosa and Bernhard, who had them detained. The women paid a fine of eight dollars and took the train back south, saying that Kennett was not the ritzy summer resort they thought they were coming to (*Free Press,* June 6–8, 1900).

Other help presumably was found without much fuss, or at least nothing reached the big ears of the local paper. But, Bernhard had other annoying troubles. In August, he was charged with maintaining a nuisance—running sewage in the street. The case was tried before a jury in Redding on August 16, 1900. Bernhard was found guilty and admonished to clean up the nuisance. It is no wonder that Rosa took to bed with a severe attack of neuralgia, an event also duly reported in the papers.

Kennett might have been small and remote, but life for its citizens was like living in a fish bowl. Absolutely everything was in the news!

The sewage was not the only problem. In a mining community such as Kennett there were many more men than women and prostitution was considered essential to order and prosperity. According to Goldmann, regulation of prostitution "emphasized the respectable community's behavioral boundaries, and heightened solidarity among respectable women" (quoted in *Limerick,* 1987, p. 51). Many of the prostitute's so-called cribs were built on stilts. It was not unusual to see occupants during the day planting a small garden or feeding some chickens on the ground under the raised buildings (Balma, 1991). This charming domestic vignette belied the sordid truth about prostitution in Western towns. Most prostitutes led grim lives, barely able to earn enough money to keep themselves alive. Suicide frequently was a prostitute's only way out.

The Golinsky family lived in the "good" part of town, in a pleasant two-story house above the hotel. It was located on the back or uphill side. It had a porch with a fine view of the Sacramento River and the surrounding mountains, and later, of course, the Mammoth Smelter. The existence of this other community and its meaning was lost on the young Rubie, as we shall see. By 1899 Kennett was growing and on the very edge of its rush into a boomtown. A great deal of planning was taking place, ready to burst forth. Local transportation was still largely by wagon, stage, or horseback, and "the way out" for those who could afford a ticket was the railroad.

My mother, Rubie, learned to ride a horse and often rode or was driven by wagon to the mines. Some of the tales I remember date from her earliest days in Kennett. She had many recollections of people getting killed by the train. Frequently, these were individuals who were drunk, but some seemed to have been deliberate. She related that:

> The tracks ran right through the town. We used to walk on them and next to them all the time. Aunt Rosa and Uncle Ben warned us very emphatically to stop, look, and listen! This seemed sensible, but it was surprising how many people paid no attention. During my early stay at Kennett, I saw a man walking along the track on the far side. He looked as if he was going to try to jump over the tracks in front of the train. People were yelling at him not to jump, but he did and he was hit by the train and killed. (Radzinski, 1926)

My mother told me Aunt Rosa's sister, Rebecca, lived in her own room in the hotel. She also told me:

> Rebecca did the dressmaking and other sewing and rather frightened me. She was very curt and severe in her conversation. I can remember how surprised I was to learn that a man, a former suitor of Rebecca's, was coming through Kennett on the train. He had written to Rebecca and gave the time of his arrival and said that he would like to see her. One day, this man arrived on the train, got off, and waited to see Aunt Rebecca. She was upstairs dressing for the occasion. Always a slow and fussy dresser, she succeeded in taking such a long time that the gentleman had to reboard the train and proceed to San Francisco without seeing Rebecca.

Now, this was one story that even as a child I found hard to believe. Forget the part that this disagreeable older woman could have had a suitor and one that wanted to see her at all! There was the business about seeing her between trains. As a small child I was used to riding on trains and I knew very well that when a train stopped at a small station, the train would pause for a very short time. A few people got off; a few people got on and off it went. For this gentleman to think that he would have a few moments to see and speak with Rebecca, and that it would be such a big deal that she would spend too much time getting ready, did not seem to ring true.

The explanation for all this came to light for me many years later while reading through the daily papers of that time. The trains stopped at Kennett at certain times of the day so that the passengers could have meals. The trains did not carry dining cars. Dining car service was not installed until October 20, 1921. Before that, one of the most popular places for a lunch or dinner was the Kennet Hotel whose dining room was famous for miles around as a place to find wonderful food and was conveniently located just across the tracks. Aunt Rebecca's friend most likely had been told this, so he expected that he would have thirty to forty-five minutes in Kennett to meet with her. This makes the story credible, but it certainly emphasized how eccentric Aunt Rebecca was.

I remember being amazed by this episode: my mother said, "one day when I was out riding, I saw a rattlesnake. He coiled up and it seemed as if he would strike me. So, I got off my horse and picked up a large rock and crushed him." For myself, I had been taught to avoid snakes and if an encounter occurred, to leave in a hurry. Either my mother was incredibly brave or incredibly foolish. Items in the local papers related similar confrontations with people who took the same action as Rubie. It seems that this method of getting rid of rattlers was a local custom!

The most exciting and vital local news was of course about mining. Local papers even carried many articles about the Alaskan Gold Rush. Jake Golinsky had a young friend, Hubert B. Porter, who had spent a year panning gold on the beaches of Nome, Alaska. He was enthusiastic about the ease of sifting gold out of the sand; no expensive machinery was needed. Porter and Jake had once been partners at Angeles Camp, California. Herbert's mother, Grace H. Porter, was known to be an "intimate friend of Mrs. B. Golinsky," according to family lore. She and her son returned from Alaska on the steamer, *Bertha,* and spent the winter in Kennett.

Many letters were received by her from Nome, with full and sometimes accurate descriptions of terrain, including the fact that on July 10, 1889, the creeks had not yet thawed enough to be worked. Even Charles Butters went up to Nome from Kennett, looking for a location suitable for a pumping plant which, however, he never established.

In the previous two years great interest had been shown in the discoveries in the Klondike. Many miners, disappointed in their California work, left for the north. Most of these returned later, sadder and wiser, but definitely not richer than when they left. Despite the glowing publicity given to mining in the Yukon and Alaska, it seemed most California people with mining interests stayed in California.

The earliest miners in Shasta County had been gold seekers. Their explorations in the fields of precious metals grew out of the Gold Rush of 1849. These miners worked streams all through northern California, usually tearing the landscape to pieces, working their claims to depletion, and then moving on to new fields. These gold miners left no settlements behind to prosper, only "ghost towns" and a ravaged environment.

It began to appear that the real wealth of Shasta County was copper. The mining of copper is a very different story from gold panning. Large numbers of people were required to work the mines, including engineers and others with some knowledge of construction and transportation. Smelters and a means of transporting the ore had to be constructed. The large number of people needed to do the mining and work the smelter and the trams meant that housing would have to be built, and communities would arise. This type of Western town became a stable place, as workers brought their families.

Churches and schools soon followed. These more civilizing elements did not do away with other aspects of mining towns:

saloons, brothels, and gambling houses. These were similar to those of earlier transient towns and flourished as well. Copper towns were destroying the environment in their own fashion. This time by smelter fumes that also ravaged the countryside, as we shall see in the story of Keswick.

Chapter 6

Keswick: The Smoky Metropolis

By 1893, Shasta County had developed into one of the major copper mining areas of the United States. Prosperity engendered by this industry was illustrated by the rapid growth of the town of Keswick and the subsequent, even greater, growth of Kennett. Part of this prosperity was related to the building and use of smelters, causing pollution, which provided a downside to the prosperity and growth. The Mountain Copper Company completed its smelter in Keswick in 1896.

During the 1890s, Kennett continued to grow, but the rate of growth had slowed considerably. The real action was taking place a few miles south and east of Kennett, at a place called Keswick (pronounced Kezzick), located near the Iron Mountain Mine. The activity had started when a well-capitalized British Company, the Mountain Copper Company, purchased the rights to the Iron Mountain tract and proceeded to build the first smelter in Shasta County. The company also built the Iron Mountain Railroad to bring ore from the mines to the smelter. Many small houses sprang up to house the workers on these ventures.

Keswick is said to have been named for Lord William Keswick of London. The town had an electric plant by late 1895 and included a section called South Park located near the smelter.

Local residents did not use the South Park designation, but referred to the whole area as Keswick.

The Mountain Copper Company built a boarding house for forty or more workers, shops, company offices, a hospital, staff houses, family cottages, all on its own land, as well as the smelter itself. In 1896, a group of forty English bachelors arrived to take up quarters in the boarding house and worked as the staff members of the mining company. The Englishmen brought with them many elements of their home country, including a rigid caste system. This was implemented in detail, including the painting of houses: white for the staff and red for the common employees. The earl of Renwick, a bonafide nobleman, was employed in the cashier's department. The Englishmen soon had created a billiard room, a reading room, and planned and gave staff balls, which were said to have been well attended by young ladies from Redding, Kennett, Anderson, and Shasta. A cricket and rugby team, as well as lawn tennis and fox hunting, were introduced.

Many Kennett businessmen were quick to notice the excitement in Keswick. Nor was this lost on Bernhard Golinsky and family. By 1896, Bernhard had built a branch store and a small hotel in Keswick. Young Jake, his nephew, moved to Keswick to manage the new store and for a while, his cousin Emil assisted in the family endeavors. Friends from Kennett were brought along to enjoy the prosperity. Jake's friend, William Schoonover, came to Keswick to work as a bookkeeper in the new Golinsky Hotel. It had a well-known dining room managed by Ben Smithson and his grandmother, Bernhard's friends from Kennett.

Post offices were established both at Keswick (near the railroad) and at South Park. This latter office was established under the name of Taylor, in honor of Clay W. Taylor, former Shasta County district attorney and state senator. The Taylor Post Office opened May 18, 1897, and the first postmaster was Jake Golinsky. Shortly, Jake also became the Wells Fargo agent, the Postal Telegraph agent, and was confirmed as a postal money

Jake Golinsky, postmaster, in Taylor Post Office, opened May 18, 1897. (Courtesy of Golinsky family)

order officer. He followed the tradition established by his older brother, Charley, in Kennett.

On plat maps, the original Keswick consisted of the railroad station and *chicken house,* and the original post office was at the station a mile or more from the real town. Through efforts of Postmaster Golinsky, the superintendent of railway mail service ordered the postal clerks to put papers and letters from the Taylor Post Office in a separate sack for more efficient delivery to the Taylor Post Office.

The Taylor Post Office was located in Jake's store, which carried general merchandise. Jake enjoyed a lively life in Keswick. While the Englishmen carried on with cricket and polo, Jake, his older brother Charley, and the non-British residents of the town enjoyed fierce competition in baseball. Jake played shortstop for Kennett and later for Keswick while he lived there. Charley played right fielder or pitcher for Kennett and, later, when he moved to San Francisco, he played for the California Marshals. He was signed as a temporary player in the position of pitcher for Weaverville in the fall of 1897.

Uncle Bernhard bought a residential lot in Keswick for Jake. In June of 1897, cousin Emil married Miss Esther Schwartz of San Francisco, who had been entertained previously in Kennett. By the end of the year Emil officially withdrew from the Golinsky Company. Life in the smoky metropolis of Keswick apparently was not enjoyed by the newly married couple, who settled in San Francisco.

Emil had not been the only local young man courting in San Francisco. Jake himself was busy in this manner. His frequent trips to San Francisco resulted in his marriage on January 17, 1898, to Miss Flora Rich, which was celebrated in San Francisco at the home of her parents. The date, January 17, was chosen to honor Bernhard and Rosa Golinsky of Kennett, whose twenty-eighth wedding anniversary was on that date. An invitation to all friends of the Golinsky family to attend the ceremony was printed in the Redding *Free Press*. There is no record to indicate how

Newly married Jake and Flora entertain Rosa and Bernhard in their Keswick home. (Courtesy of Golinsky family)

many accepted this invitation, but there is no doubt that Jake was a very popular figure locally. Jake brought his bride home to a newly finished house in Keswick, located just west of the Golinsky store.

The prosperity at Keswick was felt throughout the entire area. The Iron Mountain and the Uncle Sam mines were being worked, and many men were employed. The flux, a compound used to promote the mixture of metals, was provided for the Keswick smelter at least in part by lime rock from the Holt and Gregg Company quarries at Backbone near Kennett. Engineers and workers were employed building a tramway to convey ore from the mine to the roasters at the smelter.

Keswick quickly became known as the Smokey City or Little Pittsburgh. Sulfur smoke blanketed the town. The local papers attempted to downplay the unpleasantness, relating, "There are probably not more than a dozen days a year when we suffer any inconvenience from the smoke, and then only a few hours" (*Free Press,* February 23 1898).

Money was more important than smoke. Businesses of all kinds were flourishing, "No Rose without a Thorn, No Keswick without Smoke" (*Free Press,* June 3, 1898). The newly married Jake and Flora seemed to have settled down, accepting the good and the bad. Their little house was fairly lavishly appointed and they received a steady stream of family and friends from Kennett and San Francisco.

Smoke and sulfur fumes were disagreeable and unhealthy, but the real menace to Keswick was fire. Disastrous fires were a common occurrence in all Western boomtowns. All buildings were built of wood, most used oil lanterns, and few had any adequate water supply to fight fires. This was evident in the fire of May 12, 1898.

Early Thursday morning of May 12, 1898, fire swept through the central sections of Keswick. In one hour all the buildings on one block of Main Street were destroyed, except for the Menzel

Bros. butcher shop. There was no water supply, no fire company, no hook and ladder company, not even a bucket brigade! Fortunately there was no wind and the fire burnt itself out. The annex to the Golinsky Hotel was destroyed, but the main structure was miraculously saved and Flora and Jake's new home was not touched. Despite the fires and the smoke and unsanitary pollution from sewage, Keswick had a building boom. One hundred and nine houses were built in the year 1900 alone. Among these buildings was a new twenty-four room lodging house built by Jake Golinsky (*Free Press,* January 19, 1901). Growth continued despite the smelter fumes, which had by 1900 denuded the surrounding countryside of all vegetation except buckeye and poison oak. The air in town frequently was so smoky that it was healthier to stay indoors. These terrible conditions were referred to by the local papers as "bothersome" (*Free Press,* February 25, 1899).

The water, too, was dangerous, containing effluent from manure piles and cesspools. Physicians urged all to boil their water before using it. But the economy prospered. In 1898, the Mountain Copper Company fired up a new matte furnace, which increased the percentage of copper ore for the company, as it increased the fumes damaging to vegetation and people. From 1896, when the Keswick smelter had been built, until 1907, when it stopped production, the Mountain Copper Company prospered. It had become the largest copper producer in California, the ninth largest in the world.

From a tiny post office address, Keswick had grown to the second largest community in Shasta County. That small post office had become more efficient when, in 1899, the postmaster, Jake Golinsky, had persuaded the U.S. government to give Keswick more frequent deliveries and to discontinue the useless post office at the railroad station. Now all Keswick mail went directly to the Taylor Post Office, greatly pleasing postmaster Golinsky and the town's residents.

Despite this prosperity, complaints about fumes from the smelter grew. Small farmers, fruit growers, and then the U.S. government entered the battle against the smelter. The Mountain Copper Company was being sued constantly for damages. To settle small matters quickly, the company frequently had paid outright claims of small farmers or purchased their land from them. But if the claims were larger the cases came up in either the Shasta County courthouse or in federal court in San Francisco. For many years, every suit brought to trial by a small farmer was defeated. Juries seemed to feel that the prosperity brought by the mining companies was more important than the complaints of farmers.

The United States government had become involved in the controversy as early as 1898. In February 1906, after many years of litigation, red tape, and investigations, the U.S. Circuit Court of Appeals in San Francisco issued a permanent injunction against the Mountain Copper Company smelter at Keswick. As a result, the company dismantled the smelter, which they moved to Martinez, California. They kept the mine in operation.

During the period of litigation against the Mountain Copper Company of Keswick, the town itself continued to have problems. The air and water situation was deteriorating. There were increasing numbers of robberies and other violence, especially right after payday at the mine. And fires dealt Keswick some bad blows.

The first fire in 1897, as reported earlier, was fairly small and controlled. But, in August of 1906 a major fire began in the Keswick Hotel, owned by J. N. Stephenson, and spread throughout most of the town. Just a year later in November of 1907, the second half of the business center burned. By this date, much of the population already had left, due to the closing of the smelter. Keswick definitely was going downhill.

In the meantime, Jake Golinsky had made his own assessment of Keswick. By 1905 he had resigned his position as postmaster, sold his business and his house. He moved his family back to Kennett. He and his wife Flora now had a son, Lloyd, born 1899. The ever-helpful Uncle Bernhard made Jake the host and manager of the large new Kennet Hotel. Jake was on hand to help with the rebuilding after Kennett's fire of December 1904, and spurred the organization of a voluntary fire brigade. He built his family a new house up the hill from the Kennet Hotel.

Chapter 7

The Copper Belt: The Mammoth and Golinsky Mines

Bernhard Golinsky's first order of business when he had arrived in Kennett had been to see to the comfort and economic security of all the members of his family. First, he had established Charles in Kennett and provided enough capital to keep up the establishments and their many branches (e.g. horses, ferry boats, hauling wagons, etc.) as prosperous concerns. As noted earlier, he saw to it that Jake and his bride were comfortable in Keswick with a cozy home and an income from a store and rooming house. Charles had moved on, settling in San Francisco. His place in the store and other businesses in Kennett was taken over by the last nephew to arrive, Ben Jr., the eldest of Rosa's sister Henrietta's six children.

With the daily routines of the various businesses so well taken care of, Bernhard took the time to explore the area around Kennett and look for minerals. It would have been hard to have lived in this area and not have become caught up in the search for some form of mineral wealth. Within a few years of settling in Kennett, Bernhard had begun hiking around the countryside. Many large mines and claims were already in place, but the mineral wealth was so vast that much was still there to be discovered.

The area around Kennett was part of an extremely rich copper area. The first ores mined in Shasta County averaged seven percent copper, but sometimes ran up to fifteen percent. Today's average copper ore contains less than one percent of copper content (Kristophers, 1973). This area of Shasta County was later referred to as the Copper Belt or the Copper Crescent (Elliot, 1991). It was about thirty miles in length with a width of one half to four miles, containing massive sulfide ore. The city of Redding, near the western end of the belt, was just south of the arc. Among the large mines already located within this arc were the Iron Mountain mines near Keswick. There was renewed interest in the Uncle Sam, formally a gold mine, on the south side of Squaw Creek and the Balaklala group of mines located in the drainage basin of Squaw Creek and near the smelter at Coram.

The Golinsky claims were made in the middle of the crescent. This was the same ore body containing the Mammoth Mine, and the claims were separated from it only by Little Backbone Creek (Kinkel, 1956). The Golinsky mines, though relatively modest producers, were being worked for at least three years before the Mammoth Mine began its major operations. The main product of the Golinsky and other neighboring mines was copper, even though the ore masses contained a good percentage of gold and silver.

Exploring this area was hard work, as the canyons and rising mountains were very steep-sided. There were very few, if any, flat spots or small ledges to stand on in order to gain foothold. The first areas explored by Bernhard, often with his nephew Jake as a companion, lay at the southern end of the district. The first claims filed by them were in 1895, in the Flat Creek mining district between Motion and Coram (Shasta County Recorder, Mining Claims, Book E, p. 184 ff).

In March of 1896, Bernhard purchased from A. F. Ross a series of quartz mines located in township 34 N, 6W, section 36, known as the Snyder, Last Chance, Ridge, and Clipper mines (Shasta County Recorder, ALIMC, Book 44, p. 28). In September of the same year, he filed for the Scorpion quartz mine in the Backbone district (Shasta County Recorder, ALIMC, Book 45, p. 362). The same month, he invested some money in the active Uncle Sam Mine near Squaw Creek, where a new ledge had been discovered.

Not only was the mineral wealth topographically difficult to locate, but once found and mined, it showed another difficult or rebellious quality. It was difficult to separate the elements by smelting. Major John F. Lyons, formerly of the Confederate Army, now living in Churntown, Shasta County, owned many mining claims. His son, William, came to Kennett to work at the Mammoth Mine. Major Lyons addressed the state legislature many times, beginning around 1893, urging the state to offer to pay a $100,000 bonus to whomever could invent a process to work what he called "our rebellious ores" (*Free Press,* February 18,1893).

The difficulty in smelting the ore was caused by a high percentage of zinc blend. But, as mentioned earlier, the copper content of the early ores mined in Shasta County was exceptionally high, running from six to fifteen percent. In addition, it averaged about three dollars worth of gold and silver in each ton.

Difficult ores or not, mining claims in Shasta County were recorded on almost a daily basis. On August 3, 1899, fifty-five claim notices were filed in one day! Five of these claims were located within the Backbone district. This was the area just west of Kennett and became the area where Bernhard explored more frequently.

A corollary to mining activity was the development of limestone quarries, one of the largest being the Holt and Gregg limestone quarries at Kennett. Limestone was used as flux in the smelting of ores. The Holt and Gregg limestone quarries were reached by a good wagon road from Kennett. The road followed Backbone Creek and then passed underneath the high railroad bridge spanning the creek. It continued up the creek for about a mile and one half to a large stone abutment containing the lime kilns. The kilns were constructed in a "pot" pattern. Wood was used to fire the limestone and burn out the lime. The cooled lime was then hauled by wagon to Kennett where it was stored in a warehouse next to the railroad.

The limestone itself was hacked out of the mountain by men using pickaxes. The local limestone was considered of unsurpassed quality. Daily takes averaged about thirty tons. Two, four-horse teams were used to take the lime to the shipping point where it went by rail to the Mountain Copper Company at Keswick. Many of the four-horse teams were leased from the Golinsky Company.

An interesting sidelight is that these limestone deposits originally had been opened up by Colonel James Scobie, the expert and colorful culvert-builder for the railroad. He had carved into the limestone deposits to find material for his culverts. The land on which the quarry stood had been owned by the Southern Pacific Company, and the Holt and Gregg Company bought it from them.

As the mining claims grew, Bernhard Golinsky's name became increasingly associated with two other prospectors. One was Matt Clendenin, a younger man who was half Wintu; his mother was Native American. The other man was a boarder at the Kennet Hotel, a native of Germany, named Fritz Weischmann. He had lived at the hotel for several years and was, by 1898, considered a part of the family.

In 1898, these claims in the Backbone Mining District were recorded, listing the claimants and the names of the proposed mines:

March 15: Fritz Weischmann, Bumble Bee
March 15: B. Golinsky, Summit, quartz mine
March 31: B. Golinsky, F. Weischmann, M. Clendenin, United States, Union Gausen, and Dump
August 20: Fritz Weischmann, Interview and North Star
August 20: B. Golinsky, Good Hope and Puzzle
August 20: Matt Clendenin, Pennsylvania and Bonanza (ALIMC, Book 3, p. 84–87)

These twelve and one-half claims all were located within Sections 28 and Sections 33, range 34 N, 5 W, along Little Backbone Ridge. The following year, a fourth person, William Kemp, located three claims in this area: Ricketts, Channing, and Adolph. William Kemp sold these three claims to the group of Clendenin, Golinsky, and Weischmann in September 1899. (*Shasta County Recorder,* ALIMC, Book 3, p. 84 ff).

The Golinsky group of mines were relatively small properties within the larger Copper Crescent area. But, they were very important. At one time or another in the years following their discovery, most of the Golinsky mining claims were worked. The Golinsky group of mines became the major ore producers for the Golinsky family, although they were minor producers compared to the giants in the area such as the Balaklala, Mammoth, and Iron Mountain (Kinkel et al., 1956).

One of the twelve and one half claims was named the United States Gausen. It was the major producer of the Golinsky group. As the years passed, it was usually referred to as the Golinsky Mine. Improvements were installed in 1901 and exploratory mining was in progress by 1902.

Originally the Golinsky Mine had been reached by a pack trail that, over the years, was enlarged to a wagon road (Elliot, 1991). The road started in the town of Kennett and led to the Holt and Gregg limestone quarry. From there, it followed Little Backbone Ridge another two miles and then dropped down to the mines.

The road remained a hazardous trip. Some maps of the area show the tramway to the limestone quarry extending up the mountain to the Golinsky mines. No other reference backs up the existence of a tramway. This seems to have been wishful thinking. Some buildings and improvements were built at the mines in 1901, and by then ore was being extracted from the United States Gausen Mine.

My mother, Rubie, recalled visiting the mines at about this time. When Bernhard noticed her hiking up the hill, he felt it was too dangerous a place for her and had one of his wagon drivers take her down the mountain in a horse-driven wagon. Unknown

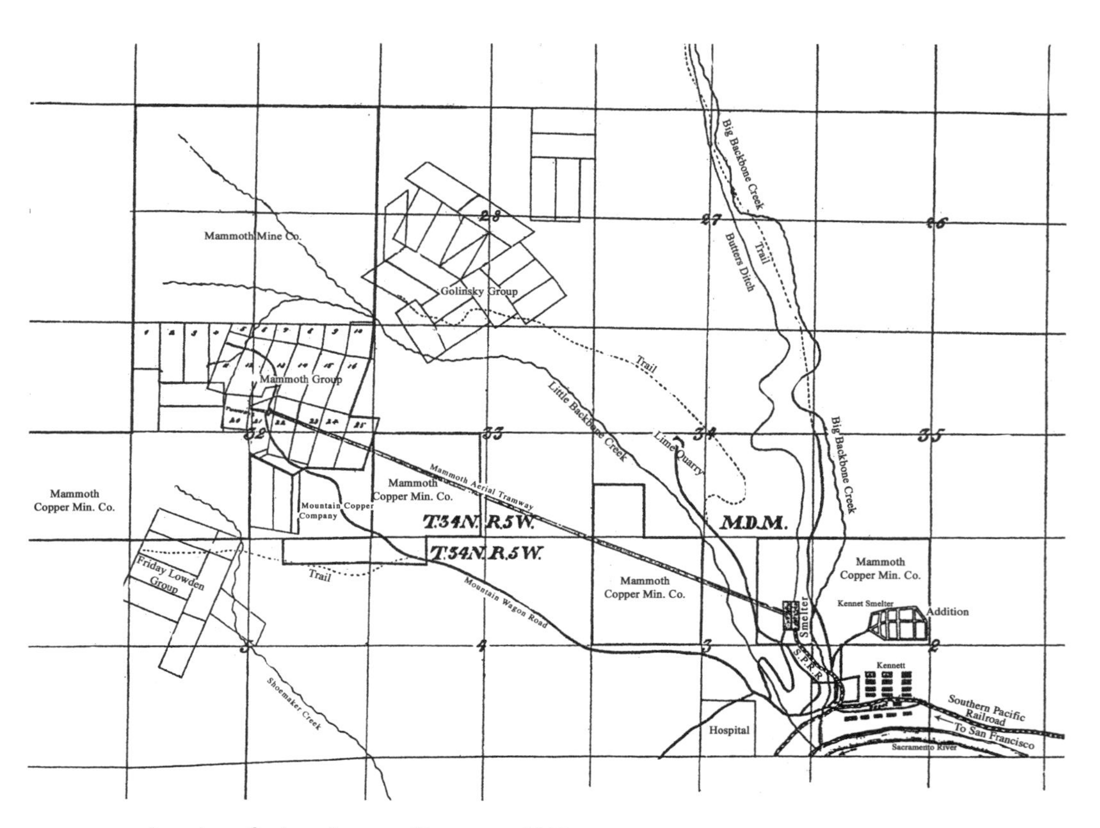

Location of mines closest to Kennett, c. 1909.

to Uncle Bernhard, the driver was very drunk and he reportedly took perverse pleasure in whipping the horses and driving the wagon perilously close to the edge as they sped down the mountain. At the base of the hill, the wagon was slowed down by a group of young miners who vaulted on the horses and grabbed the reins. The blushing heroine is reported to have smiled at her rescuers. The driver was subsequently fired. However, runaway wagons were fairly common (*Free Press,* September 12 and September 25, 1908).

No attempt was made at this early date to smelt the ore at the site. The location of the Golinsky Mine was on a slope so steep that building any large structure was impossible. In 1903 about $1,600 were invested in labor and improvements (*Shasta County Recorder,* ALIMC, Book 2, p. 170). In the following five years, similar amounts were spent on the mines, almost all at the United States Gausen Mine. In 1908, $1,700 were invested. At this time, the labor affidavit was signed by W. D. Tillotson. This was the start of his long-term association with the Golinskys. Similar amounts of money were invested in 1916.

As the area began to be explored and opened up, the general sense of prosperity and copper fever grew. Word of this activity reached the giant companies in the East. During 1906–1907, the Golinsky Mine was bonded (a type of lease on a mine dependant on specific results before it is either dropped or turned into a purchase) by the American Smelting and Refining Company, owned by the Lewisohn family of New York.

The Mammoth group on Little Backbone Creek was also bonded by Lewisohn Brothers, copper brokers from New York City. The Golinsky-Clendenin group was being developed by a group of twenty or more miners, supervised by William Kemp who was an employee of Lewisohn Brothers. The Golinsky-Clendenin group was bonded for $130,000 in February of 1899. This property consisted of the twelve and one-half mining claims on Little Backbone Creek and 320 acres of land. An additional

Above and next page: The Golinsky Mine property c. 1898. (Courtesy of United States Department of Interior)

$30,000 bond was taken by Lewisohn Brothers for various other sites and water rights. Lewisohn's bond on the Golinsky group was for one year. By July, the miners working under William Kemp had tunneled 200 feet below the surface, attempting to cross a ledge thought to contain the richest ore. In August, Lewisohn Brothers sent out an agent, J. Park Channing, to inspect the work and give his opinion. Mr. Channing decided that the results of the development work would not seem to justify the purchase price of $160,000 stipulated in the bond. The work was discontinued and the bond was dropped.

During the same period of time, Golinsky–Clendenin–Weischmann were sued by Colonel A. C. Ellis, who claimed that each of these three owners had verbally given him a contract for one-fourth interest in the Golinsky group of mines. The case came to Superior Court in Redding in September of 1899. By this time, Lewisohn Brothers had already withdrawn their bond. With this knowledge in hand, the attorney for Colonel Ellis asked for a dismissal of the case. This attorney was W. D. Tillotson,

before he become intimately involved with the Golinsky family. This case that he argued, which was against the Golinskys, seems to be the first mention of Mr. Tillotson's association with the Golinskys. He later became an associate of the family.

There can be no doubt that Bernhard and his partners were disappointed by Lewisohn's decision to withdraw their bond. Officially, Bernhard kept up his optimism. He seemed to have had the large share of the sense optimism and the high expectation of all new settlers, who expected the West to deliver. In December 1899, he was interviewed by the Redding *Free Press*. He spoke glowingly of prospects and indicated that he had other buyers interested in the Golinsky group.

It was reported that over 3,000 tons of sulfide ore from the Mammoth mines were shipped to the ASARCO (American Smelting and Refining Company) smelter in Tacoma, Washington, and that the Lewisohns planned to ship 100 tons of ore per day. In order to handle such large amounts of ore, plans were made to extend the Holt and Gregg narrow gauge line from the quarry up the mountain to the mine. As mentioned earlier, this never happened and mule power continued to be the main form of transport. Such large amounts of ore encouraged the Mammoth Company to build their own smelter. By far the most important mining activity in Shasta County was the reopening of Mammoth Mine and the building and operation of the Mammoth Smelter located on the west side of the Sacramento River. The mine itself was located just south and west of the town of Kennett, between Mammoth Butte and Little Backbone Creek at 3,000 feet of elevation. The mine had been located around 1882 by a Mr. Frazier and mined fairly extensively for gold by a Mr. Nelson. It was again worked in 1885 by Harry Wyman, who abandoned it. The mine then was worked by William Nichols of Copley, California.

In 1896, the mine was bonded for one year to William Jackson, who at that time was treasurer of Shasta County. He abandoned his work just a few yards short of the main copper vein. In 1897, George Graves, who was one of the original owners, sold his interest to a group from Redding made up of R. M. Saeltzer, Antone Jaegel, A. J. Wallace, and Joseph A. Kahny. This group did more exploration and some work. Word of this activity reached the East. In 1904 Mammoth Mine was purchased by United States Smelting Refining and Mining Company, which formed the Mammoth Copper Mining Company. This company operated between 1904 and 1919.

The Mammoth Company began to build its smelter at its chosen site in August 1901. This smelter went ahead despite the legal action which had closed down Iron Mountain Smelter at Keswick. The first buildings constructed in the Mammoth complex were the wooden machine shop, bunkhouses, mess house, and tool sheds. At the same time, ground was broken for the smelter itself. The smelter was built on a steep hill, and thus, a two-level plan was used. The upper level of the smelter was built to house the concrete bins to hold lime, silica, and ore. These bins were located just below the new upper railroad track. The blowers and engines also were located on this level. The blast furnaces were located on the lower level, fed by material from the upper level and loaded into cars on the lower railroad spur. By early 1906, three blast furnaces on this level were ready to be blown. Kristophers (1973) provides a very detailed analysis of the smelter operations.

The first furnace was blown in October 1905. This was in reality a "ceremonial" blowing, made to honor an agreement made with Charles Butters from whom the land for the smelter had been purchased. The agreement was for the smelter operation to start on or before October 18, 1905. This marked one year from the date that the agreement had been signed. After the ceremonial blowing, the furnace was blown out to permit the final completion of the aerial tramway that was being built to bring material from the mine to the smelter.

Mamoth smelter and smokestacks. The mine itself is located high on the mountain a little right of center. (Courtesy of Shasta Historical Society)

The second furnace was started in December 1905 and the third one in December 1906. This last furnace was ready to be blown in March of that year. The smelter was in full operation by 1905 and was enlarged in 1907. By that time, the Mammoth Smelter had surpassed the Coram Smelter and became the largest smelter on the Pacific Coast.

People were pouring into Kennett to work at the smelter and the mine. By 1905, Kennett had passed Keswick in population. The building of the smelter, company offices, and workers' houses was clearly visible to all of Kennett. With the blowing of the third furnace at the Mammoth Smelter in March 1906, work at the smelter proceeded on a twenty-four hour basis. Work at the smelter was hot, noisy, and dangerous, but it was steady and well paid. By 1907, there were 800 men working at the smelter in three shifts, and the monthly payroll reached $1,000,000.

In June, the Mammoth Company added to its dining room that had previously seated 312. With the addition it was able to serve ninety-six more. It was heated in the winter. Twenty-one people worked in the kitchen. At this time there were seventy-five families working in the camp and thirty-five new cottages were being built. The Mammoth Copper Company established a new wage scale, raising the pay of all of its workers and establishing an eight-hour workday for both miners and smelter workers. The company was widely praised and respected for its treatment of its workers (*Free Press,* January 16, 1907).

On December 1, 1899, Fritz Weischmann, Bernhard's partner and a family friend, was killed by the northbound California Express. He had tried to jump across the track in front of the train, even though several people, among them my mother, yelled for him not to attempt it. This dramatic event was part of my mother's memories of her early life in Kennett as mentioned earlier.

Weischmann was fatally injured in his collision with the train, and he died a few hours later at the Golinsky Hotel, where he had been residing for the past fourteen years. He was fifty-six years old, a bachelor, and, as noted previously, was from Germany. He had become almost a part of the Golinsky family. During his last hours he dictated his will to the doctor in attendance, Dr. Fraser. He appointed C. G. Ferguson as his executor. He was buried in Kennett. The funeral arrangements were made by Bernhard, and many kind words were said about him at the graveside.

A week later, Weischmann's will was filed for probate and the heirs were revealed. They were his brother, Antone, in Germany, Dr. Fraser, and my mother, Miss Ruby [*sic*] Radzinski, the niece of B. Golinsky! This last piece of news must have come as a shock to the family and perhaps to my mother as well. It seemed likely that Miss Rubie was polite and kind to the lonesome, older man and probably listened to his stories of the old country and his service in the German army (Franco-Prussian War). It seemed very unlikely that there was any, however innocent, form of courtship. Aunt Rosa would most likely have noticed this and put a stop to it. Whatever his gesture meant, we will never know. As for the estate, very little was left after debts were paid.

Weischmann's remaining interest in the mines was purchased by Bernhard. This transaction was recorded in the *Shasta County Book of Deeds* in July 1900 and was accomplished by Bernhard at an open sale of Weischmann's assets. No further reference is made to Weischmann's verbal, deathbed request that Miss Ruby [*sic*] Radzinski receive one third of his estate. Since she was underage, Bernhard took care of matters and promised Rubie a share when she came of age. It is important however, to note that nothing was bequeathed to her when Bernhard died in 1914. She did, however, receive a large amount of stock from the reorganized Golinsky Copper Company when Rosa died in 1932. This will be discussed in greater detail later in the next chapter.

Chapter 8

Other Prospering Mines and Smelters

While family interests centered on the Golinsky mines, a great deal more activity was taking place in the nearby mining districts in the larger claims. Bernhard kept himself informed on the activity and sometimes became an important player. In January 1899, the Uncle Sam Mine had been purchased by Fred H. Dakin from the Sierra Buttes Mining Company. Very little activity had taken place at the Uncle Sam in the previous few years, although a great deal of work had occurred there in the past. The Uncle Sam had long been thought to be one of the biggest producers of gold in the district. It was rumored that the other pioneer Kennett resident, Charles Butters, was somehow connected to the purchase.

Butters still owned a chlorination plant at Kennett as well as valuable water rights on Backbone Creek. In the summer of 1898, Butters started to repair and improve his chlorinating plant at Kennett, as well as repairing and extending the flume and ditch from Big Backbone Creek to bring water to the town. His name in connection with renewed activity at the Uncle Sam would have enhanced interest in the mine's potential.

In the meantime, Mr. Dakin had started improving the old Uncle Sam Mine. All the old buildings were renovated and the old stamp mill was repaired. Soon more than twenty men were employed. The Golinsky Company's daily stage line between Kennett and the mine accommodated many workers. At the same time as the renewed activity at the Uncle Sam, work also was being resumed at the Mammoth.

Despite the years of controversy about the pollution from the smelter at Keswick, its eventual dismantling and the subsequent ruin of the town of Keswick, by 1901 three new smelters were in the planning stages in the Sacramento River canyon. One of these was the Trinity Copper Company. Of great interest to all in the area was the exact location of this planned smelter.

In June 1901, Mr. and Mrs. Bernard Golinsky offered the Trinity Copper Company almost forty acres of land at no cost. (*Free Press*, June 10, 1901). This land was located one mile south of Kennett on a flat piece of land near the mouth of the smaller, southern Squaw Creek. The only conditions requested by the Golinskys were that (1) the smelter site be decided in ninety days, (2) smelting was to begin within nine months, (3) three acres of this land be set aside for use by the Golinskys, and (4) the Trinity Copper Company cover any loss to Bernhard Golinsky caused by actions of Trinity employees. Apparently, the three acres of land would be used by the Golinskys for businesses that would bring them financial remuneration. The land location was termed the SW quarter of the SE quarter of section three, Township T 33 N, 5 W, and comprised 37.38 acres of land (*Free Press,* June 10, 1901).

This seemingly too-good-to-be-true offer was never taken up by the Trinity Copper Company. The company decided not to build a smelter at all and concentrated on mining. This decision was a disappointment to many, but the Trinity Copper Company did build a fairly impressive building in Kennett on Railroad Avenue. This lot was purchased from Charles Butters and housed their offices. As the mines grew, more companies built homes and offices in Kennett. The Trinity Copper Company of Boston, Massachusetts, had come to Kennett to develop their holdings at the "Shasta King." The president was Thomas Lawson, for whom Lawson Street was named. The company also built a large office building across from the railroad station.

Located about two miles south of Kennett on the south fork of Squaw Creek was the town of Coram. It was created by the prosperity of the Balaklala Mine. The Balaklala Consolidated Copper Company was in no way deterred by the death of the town of Keswick due to the forced dismantling of its smelter. Balaklala built its own smelter at Coram and, by 1905, it had become the largest and most modern smelter on the West Coast.

An aerial tramway was constructed to connect the mine to the smelter. The smelter was run entirely by electricity and was called the Million Dollar Smelter because of its modern and impressive size (Kristophers, 1973). The builders of this smelter apparently had thought that it was located too far up the Sacramento River canyon to cause any damage to agricultural lands to the south. There was very little agriculture in the canyon itself and most of the land there was used for mining activities.

The potential wealth available for the taking provided a tempting plum. In this way, it was rationalized that a decision to build a new smelter right on the heels of the demolition of the Keswick smelter was a logical move. Evidently the owners did not cast their eyes to the landscape around Keswick and notice the denuded hills.

In 1905, the countryside just around Kennett was still agreeably green, and any qualms about smelters that might have been felt were calmed by the positive statements of a botany professor from the University of California at Berkeley, W. J. V. Osterhout. Professor Osterhout declared that smelter fumes did no harm to plants! He was backed by Professor E. O'Neill, who was head of the Department of Chemistry, also at UC, Berkeley (*Free Press,* September 16, 1906). It is presumed that neither of these gentlemen had visited the land around the abandoned smelter at Keswick.

Over the years however, the increasing use of roasters, blast furnaces, and the like caused increased smoke and sent sulfide pollutants down the valley. Around 1900 it was thought that the best way to tackle this problem was to build incredibly tall chimneys. It was hoped that smoke released high in the atmosphere would disperse widely enough to minimize the problem. The Balaklala stack at Coram was two hundred and fifty feet high and eighteen feet in diameter. This enormous structure, although impressive to the eye, did nothing to solve the pollution problem.

Paralleling the earlier situation at Keswick, the fumes from Coram caused serious damage to farm and orchard crops. Encouraged by their previous success in eliminating the smelter at Keswick, the valley farmers again banded together to protest this new source of pollution. In 1911, a suit by the Shasta County Farmers' Protective Association succeeded in closing the Coram Smelter. The mine continued to be worked until the end of World War I, with the ore being sent by train to other smelters. The town of Coram, which had grown to over two thousand people by 1908, joined Keswick in becoming an instant ghost town when its smelter was closed in 1911.

Unlike the mines and smelters in the west such as Keswick, which were shut down for air pollution, mines and smelters in the east copper zinc district were too small to draw enough attention to be shut down. The mines in the Copper Crescent discovered east of the Sacramento River were not as rich in copper as the mines located in the west. This area was called the East Shasta Copper-Zinc District (Kristophers, 1973). Deposits here were found in acidic lava flows called Balaklala rhyolite. The bodies of the ore contained pyrite, and the location of large deposits were often marked by caps of iron oxide known as gossan (Kristophers, 1973). The most important mines in this district were the Bully Hill at Dalamar-Wintrop and the Afterthought and Donkey at Ingot. The ore from these two districts contained a higher percentage of gold, copper and silver and less sulfur than the ore located in the West Shasta Copper-Zinc District (Iron Mountain, Balaklala, Mammoth, Golinsky, etc.).

Bully Hill was located about nineteen miles northeast of Redding and was on the larger, upper stream known as Squaw Creek. Communities that developed to serve Bully Hill were Ydalpom (Copper City), Delamar, and Winthrop. The Afterthought and Donkey mines were about twenty miles northeast of Redding on the east side of Little Cow Creek Canyon. The community that arose was called Ingot.

Both mining communities built smelters; the Bully Hill smelter was located at Delamar, while its workers lived next door at Winthrop. The smelter for the Afterthought and Donkey was built about a mile down the river from the town of Ingot. This was the smallest mining-smelter operation in Shasta County.

Both of these areas had experienced previous good times. The first had occurred when placer gold was found around 1853. This produced a boom and a subsequent fizzle. Then came the discovery of silver around 1862, starting another boom period. In 1889 the Bully Hill mining property was bought by Captain J. R. De La Mar, who created the Bully Hill Copper Mining and Smelting Company. He erected the smelter in the town of Winthrop. The Afterthought Mine at Ingot was purchased by the Great Western Gold Company in 1903. In 1905 a 250-ton smelter was built downstream from Ingot. In 1909 the mine and smelter were purchased by the Afterthought Copper Company.

The greatest problem facing mines in the East Shasta District was an inadequate transportation system. In March 1908 the Bully Hill Mining Company began operating a newly built railroad, the Sacramento Valley and Eastern Railroad. It ran from Bully Hill, through Delamar and Copper City, keeping on the north side of the Pit River, to a connection with the Southern Pacific at a siding called Pit, located two miles above Kennett (*Searchlight,* November 14, 1906). This railroad replaced the slow and roundabout, expensive hauling by wagons over rough roads.

Supplies for the Afterthought had to be hauled by wagons from Bellavista, which was the terminus for the Anderson and Bellavista Railway, a short line of about fifteen miles that followed a route down the valley of the Cow Creek to Anderson and a connection with the Southern Pacific. Both of these rail lines were totally dependant on successful smelter and mining operations in this district; they had not been built to be passenger or light freight operations. Some enthusiasts, however, envisioned the Bully Hill Line, eventually connecting with a transcontinental railroad, possibly the Rock Island Line (*The Searchlight,* January 19, 1906). These mines contributed to the activity and prosperity of this area.

The lapsed Trinity Smelter project was picked up by the Mammoth Company. They purchased from Charles Butters a large tract of land on the west side of Backbone Creek. It was less than half a mile from the railroad and about the same distance from the main part of Kennett. The deal included access to Butters' water rights and his five-mile long ditch from Backbone Creek (east one half of NW quarter, section three, township T 33 N, 5 W). The location of the future Mammoth Smelter was thus, settled.

Chapter 9

Growth After the Great 1904 Fire

When the Mammoth Smelter site was chosen, Charles Butters had laid out a new subdivision located between Little Backbone and Big Backbone creeks near the new smelter area. There was no doubt that a real "boom" was starting in Kennett. In late August of 1901, it was announced that Kennett was to have an opera house (*Free Press,* August 26, 1901). The project would consist of a three-story building just south of the railroad depot and on the same side of the tracks.

The lowest floor would have the theatre with a modern stage and equipment. There were also plans for a bar and restaurant. Stores would occupy the first story and thirty lodging rooms the second. The cost was estimated at $4,000. Most of this money was supplied by William Trewartha, Victor Warrens, and David Endicott. The opera house was completed and in full swing by the end of 1905. Local people heralded it as the best in Shasta County (McKim, 1985). The opera house was almost continuously booked by singers, vaudeville acts, and traveling circuses. Kennett also had a grandstand located on the upper side of Railroad Avenue between Trewartha's new drug store and the Kennet Hotel.

Also on the books was an eighteen-room addition to the one-year-old Smithson Hotel. Plans were laid for a two-story courtroom and office building, a new blacksmith shop, and another lodging house. It was time for the Golinskys to jump on the bandwagon. New projects planned by the Golinsky family included the building of a totally new, sixty plus room Kennet Hotel, expansion of the dining room, and erection of a large, new merchandise store. In addition to Butter's subdivision there was a whole new town site, located near the yet to be built Mammoth Smelter. It was to be named Bernhard for its owner/developer Bernhard Golinsky himself.

Kennett's worst disaster to date hit on Saturday morning, December 3, 1904. A fire started in J. S. Smithson's saloon, and by noon every building on the south side of the railroad tracks had burnt down. The only buildings left standing in the main section of Kennett were on the north side of the tracks: The Trinity Copper Company offices on the hill northeast of the depot, and Golinsky's store, hotel, and residence. Fortunately, the Southern Pacific Depot, though on the south side of the tracks, escaped the flames. (Fire reports from *Free Press* December 3 and December 4, 1904.)

David Endicott's two-story hotel, which had housed the offices of the Mammoth Copper Company, went down with a "smoking crash." Despite the devastation in Kennett, the Mammoth Mine and Smelter were largely unaffected by the fire. Fortunately, with help the Trinity Copper Company managed to get all of its books, papers, and its safe out of its building on Railroad Avenue. The office fixtures piled in the street soon found temporary quarters in B. Golinsky's building on the north side of the tracks.

Rebuilding occurred with amazing speed. Ashes were still piled about when Charles Butters began a new two-story building on the north side of the tracks. This building was constructed of brick, a material now regarded with new interest, although it cost too much for most people. J. N. Conant, justice of the peace,

Panoramic view of Kennett c. 1905. (Courtesy of Special Collections, Meriam Library, California State University, Chico)

rebuilt his building of wood. It was considered to represent the best architecture in the town.

Despite the speed of rebuilding, living accommodations were extremely scarce for many months. It was noted that "the sleeping accommodations overnight were so crowded that patrons must either sleep standing or stay awake walking" (*Free Press,* January 12, 1905). Golinsky's Kennet Hotel and store became the liveliest and most crowded places in town, having the only good public accommodations available. Over 150 people were boarding in the hotel, which was built to accommodate half that number. There were two beds in a room and two to three men in a bed. There were beds in the hallways and every imaginable space. According to one reporter, "The management is trying to accommodate more of their friends and patrons. Just how this is to be accom-

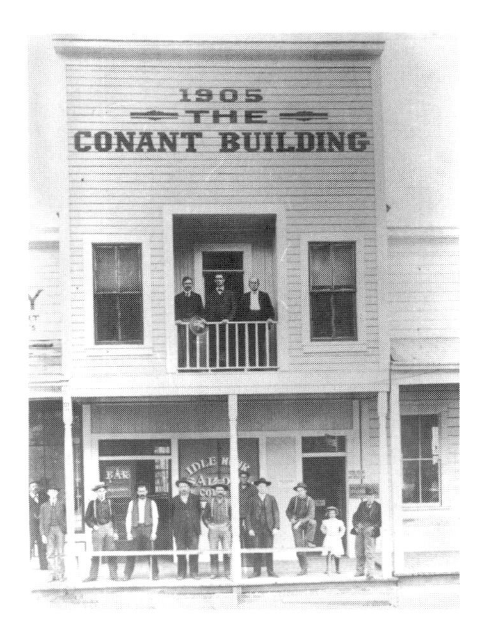

Above, Conant Building, rebuilt after the fire of 1904. (Courtesy of Shasta Historical Society)

Below, Rebuilding on Lawson Street after fire of 1904. (Courtesy of Balma family)

plished is somewhat indefinite, unless they are hung up on hooks and placed on the walls" (*Free Press,* February 10, 1905). The dining room fed more than 200 people a day. There were five waiters and a steward employed, the whole operation overseen by Mrs. Golinsky (Rosa).

The railroad station was filled each night with homeless people, many of them hobos, but also many guests who overflowed from the hotel. Supplies of every sort were piling up at the depot. In January, the Golinskys, in order to get their own necessities up the

hill, built a cart to convey freight. It was definitely not a model of beauty, but proved serviceable.

Instead of sleeping in the depot or lining the walls of the Kennet Hotel, a man could go to one of the numerous saloons being built and drink the night away. Bars were opening on a daily basis, most located on the south side of the railroad tracks. An incomplete count made by scanning newspaper reports of new saloons turned up a list of ten by February 1905, beginning with Victor E. "Slim" Warrens' Diamond Bar, located just west of the depot and on the same side of the tracks. This was a sturdily built four-story building, first of wood, but later improved with brick. As was necessary when building on this side of the tracks, only two stories showed on Railroad Avenue; the other two went down the hill in back. The Diamond Bar became the most famous building in Kennett due to its lavish décor and the colorful personality of its owner.

Beautiful weather during the first two weeks of January aided the rebuilding effort. But, on January 13 the weather changed rapidly. The wind veered to the north and six inches of snow fell within a few hours. All outdoor building work stopped, and indoor space remained as unpleasantly crowded as before. The bad weather lasted most of January. Bernhard had his sixty-third birthday on February 15, which was cheerily celebrated despite the fact that neither Rosa nor Bernhard felt very well. Both were worn out by the hectic conditions at the hotel. When a niece and nephew came by from Chicago for a visit, Ben and Rosa took the opportunity to join them in travels to San Jose and Del Monte. My mother Rubie was temporarily back in Chicago, which left the stage to the three brothers, Ben Jr., Charley, and Jake to once again oversee the multiple building projects planned on their property.

The first project was the demolition of Kennett's pioneer building, the building bought by Charley from Ollie Whitten in 1885 and added to many times since. It had been Kennett's first store, rooming house, bar, and post office, and had housed the Kennett office of the Redding *Free Press.* Before Rosa left on her vacation she had fitted up a room for the *Free Press* in the newly remodeled hotel.

The excavation and demolition of the old structures began at once, plagued by frequent cave-ins from the hill on the upper side. The frame of the new store rose in March, only to be damaged by another cave-in, after a blast on an adjoining lot went off. All was eventually repaired and the store completed. Many of the fixtures were purchased from the Mountain Copper Company's store at Taylor, sold due to the dwindling population at Keswick.

Rosa and Bernhard returned at the end of March to find a completed new store. A grand ball was given on April 1, 1905, to celebrate the opening. All were invited to attend the celebration, which included free refreshments, a band, dancing, and many pieces of fine glassware and crockery given away to guests.

Slim Warren's Diamond Bar inside and out. Man at bar is said to be Tog Balma, eldest of the large Balma family. (Courtesy of Shasta Historical Society)

Chapter 10

Bernhard: The New Town

Of all the tales told to me by my mother and bolstered by family members, the most persistent one was the information that all the streets in Kennett were named after members of the family. When I was first handed a map of Kennett at Special Collections, Meriam Library, California State University, Chico, I could hardly contain my excitement. I hastily scanned it. It was a map made by the Pacific Gas and Electric Company in 1919 to be used to identify their customers. But, what a disappointment! The streets on this map were named Kennett, Lawson, Butters, Tehama, Smelter, School, Fir, Spring, etc. No family names!

It was not until several years later when I was given plat maps of the area from the Department of Interior, Sacramento, California, that I discovered the town site of Bernhard. There, indeed, the streets were named after family members. This included one named for my mother, Rubie.

The town site of Bernhard consisted of 160 acres purchased by Bernhard from Sam Williams in 1894. It was located west of Kennett, the Sacramento River, and the Southern Pacific Railroad tracks. The *Free Press* on December 12, 1904, wrote the following about this area:

> The new town is named after Bernhard Golinsky, "the father of Kennett," and the founder of the new smelter city. This is

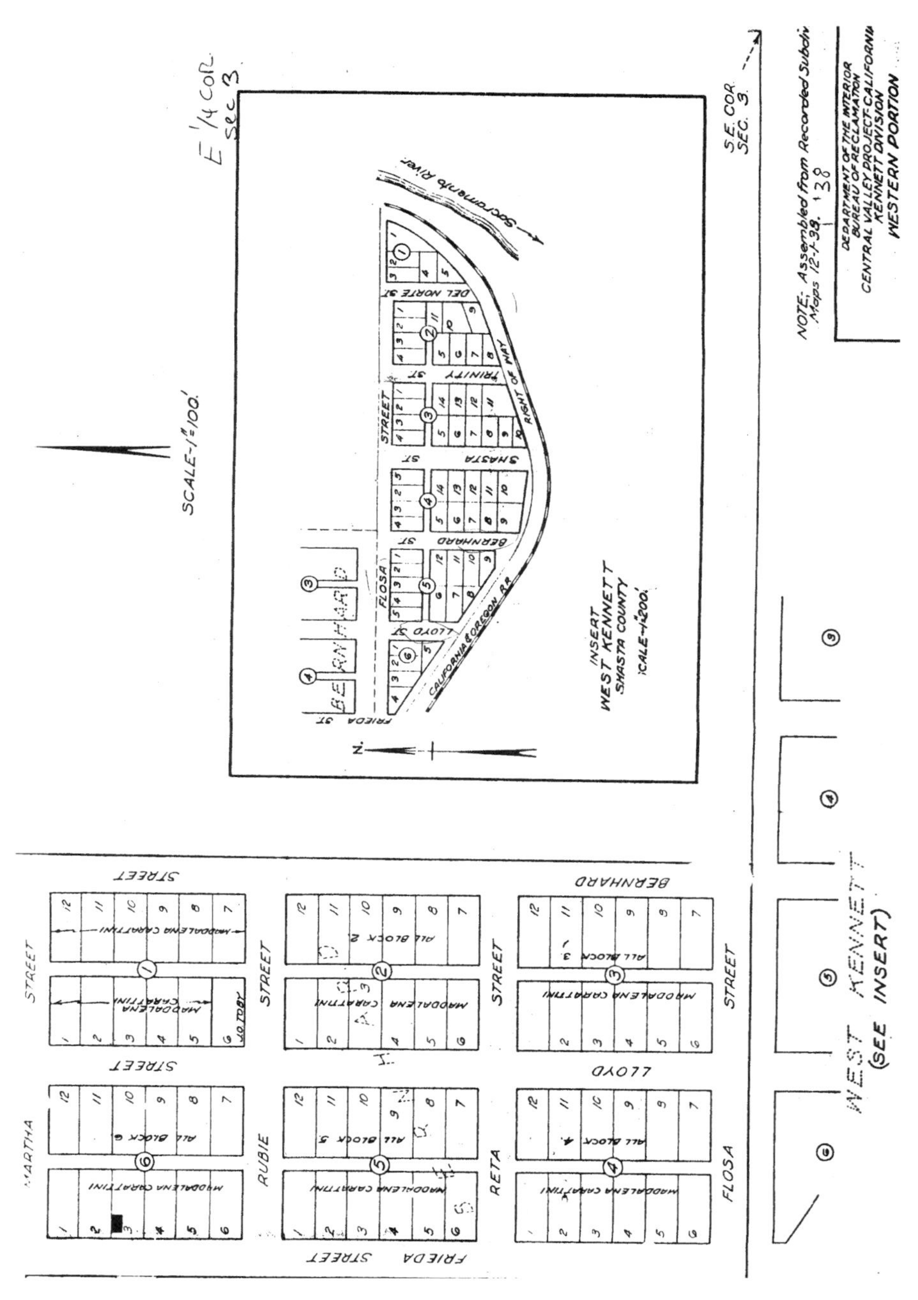

Township of Bernhard, where streets were named after family members. Note Rubie Street. Circa 1905. (Courtesy of United States Department of Interior)

> bound to grow and take its place among the progressive communities of Shasta County.
>
> Mr. Golinsky has made all the preliminary arrangements for the new smelter town. It will face the smelter and will be laid out within one-eighth mile of the plant. The new town will be three forth miles from Kennett and will be on the main line of the Southern Pacific Railroad. A siding will be laid out ... the town will be on flat land and the founder intends to make it a model for a small city. (*Free Press,* December 2, 1904)

The new town's water supply was assured by the discovery of a commodious spring about five hundred yards above the town site and on Golinsky property. It was named the Golinsky Springs. To forestall concerns about smelter smoke, a large brush fire was lit to see where the smoke would drift. With the wind blowing over the ridge from the smelter site, it was demonstrated that the new town site, according to family tales, would escape any smoke drifts.

The town was platted and graded in December 1904, and the first houses of the twenty contracted from W. G. Ewing were built in March 1905. On the north side of the property the Mammoth Company built its hospital. Bernhard had plans in hand to erect a new $10,000 hotel to be named for Mr. Frederick Lyons, the genial and well-liked manager of the Mammoth Copper Company. It was to be large, completely modern, and lighted by electricity.

An elaborate picnic and entertainment was planned to celebrate the opening of the Bernhard town site. Rosa took an active part in the planning and carrying out of the event. She made several trips down to Redding to buy decorations, including Japanese lanterns. She saw to the printing of posters advertising the event, and she persuaded the Southern Pacific Railroad to issue special round-trip tickets at the one-way fare for those

The Bernhard picnic, May 2, 1907. (Courtesy of Golinsky family)

coming to the picnic either from the north or south. Rosa designed a silk flag of red, bordered by blue, with white letters a foot high spelling "Bernhard." A large dance platform was built, as well as arbors and comfortable seats. A grandstand was built in the area and, at that time, it was tree shaded and quite lovely.

The picnic had to be postponed twice due to rainy weather. It was finally set for Sunday, May 21, 1905. The *Free Press* on May 15, 1905, carried the following report: "Mr. and Mrs. Golinsky know how to entertain and they are going to give their guests next Sunday one of the biggest times ever enjoyed in northern California." Nearly two hundred people arrived on the morning train from Redding along with the eighteen-piece Woodmen of the World band. About fifty residents of La Moine arrived from the north for the picnic and to root for their baseball team that was playing against Kennett in the afternoon.

All details were carefully attended to, such as the checking of picnic baskets and supplying vehicles from the station for those not desiring to walk to the picnic. There were speeches, dancing, walks in the woods and along the river, and the ball game. Kennett lost to La Moine. The Redding *Free Press* wrote:

> Every detail of the affair was carried out to the letter and great credit is due to Mr. and Mrs. Golinsky who got up the affair. But the grandest thing that can be said of Sunday's celebration is that not a disturbance of any kind marred the pleasures of the day, drunkenness and rowdyism [*sic*] being conspicuous by its absence a honor to Kennett and all concerned (Redding *Free Press,* May 22, 1905).

On May 12, 1905, just three days before the anticipated Bernhard picnic was to occur, the Southern Pacific Railroad stunned the entire community of Kennett. It had announced that the railroad was claiming a 200-foot right-of-way through the town. This claim threatened every property owner on Railroad Avenue. Each property located there had been built within a 100-foot radius, a figure based on the exact wording in the patent on this property issued by the United States government in 1861 to George W. Moore, the original (European) property owner. All property owned in this area in 1905, was partly located on a piece of the original Moore property.

In 1881 Mr. Moore had sold by deed to the railroad company a right-of-way 100-feet wide, that is 50 feet on either side of the tracks. By this 1881 transaction, the railroad company had tacitly recognized George W. Moore's title to the land. By the same token, the company had recognized the title to the rest of the land purchased from him by various Kennett pioneers. If the railroad claim was upheld, every building located on Railroad Avenue would be cut in half, or worse. In addition all property owners had been paying taxes on their property now claimed by the Southern Pacific; this was another indication of their established rights to the land.

Southern Pacific sent an agent to Kennett to offer the property owners leases on the ground that they occupied on the area that the railroad now claimed. The agent found no takers; in fact, he was met by a hostile crowd made up of Charles Butters and the Golinsky family who were for once on the same side of an issue. Additionally, James Smithson, W. R. Conant, E. C. Warren, Dave Endicott, Dr. Heyford, Peter Monga, and ten other property owners joined the group (Redding *Morning Searchlight,* May 12, 1905). In the face of overwhelming evidence of property rights, the Southern Pacific Railroad withdrew its claim.

At this time in 1905, public discussions were under way in Kennett about the need for a new schoolhouse. Mr. and Mrs. B. Golinsky offered to donate a level two-acre lot in the new Bernhard town site to be used for a new school and a church. The *Free Press* described this idea on January 19, 1905:

> Mrs. B. Golinsky also states that if the new school site at Bernhard is chosen she will head the subscription list with fifty dollars toward securing the necessary funds for the erection of the church buildings and that she will see that the amount subscribed reaches one thousand dollars for a place of worship. The church, says Mrs. Golinsky, must be a nonsectarian one, where all people belonging to the different denominations can go to listen or hold services. This is certainly extending liberality to the public with a generosity that bespeaks for the interest manifested in the public welfare.

The first school in Kennett had been located in a small, shed-like building on property owned by Holt & Gregg, the lime quarry company. In 1905, they gave notice to the school directors that the property was needed for business. At a meeting of the school directors in January 1905, Holt & Gregg indicated that they would erect a new school free of charge on any new lot selected by the people. As noted previously, Rosa Golinsky made

Free Press, January 25, 1905

Bernhard Lots!

Most desirable. Hardly ¼ of a mile of Mammoth Smelter. On the direct road to every mine. Ice cool, pure healthful water to every cottage from a height of 1500 feet. Choice lots from $35 up

Bernhard Golinsky
KENNET, CAL.

Redding *Free Press,* January 1907. Here Kennett is spelled with one *t*.

her generous offer of a two-acre lot in the new town site of Bernhard for the erection of a new school. Her offer of a school, as well as her visionary plan for an ecumenical house of worship, was rejected by the public as well as by the school directors. They indicated that they thought the Bernhard site was too close to the smelter and too far from the center of the Kennett residential areas. Of greater impact in this decision was the offer of a lot in the upper part of town, to be donated by Mrs. Butters Sr. This site furthered the vision of her son, Charles, in creating his model community.

When the decision was made to locate the new school at the

A $50 LOT

—IN—

Butters' Kennet Townsites

Will Return Good Money

No saloons. No smoke. Highest and healthiest part of Kennett. Adjoins smelter site. Postoffice and school adjacent. Drop a postal for full particulars.

S. M. STONE **KENNETT**

Free Press, January 25, 1905. Here Kennett is spelled with one *t* and two *t*'s.

extreme northern part of town, a group of local leaders traveled to Redding and appeared before the Shasta County Board of Supervisors on behalf of building a bridge across Big Backbone Creek. This bridge would allow the children from Bernhard and homes near the smelter as well to walk to school safely. At present they had to walk over the railroad trestle, exposing themselves to great danger. Among the advocates who went to Redding to plead for a pedestrian bridge were Bernhard Golinsky, Judge Conant, and Carl Dittmar, the newspaper man. Accordingly, the Mammoth Copper Company built a suspension bridge just above the smelter, giving the children a shorter and safer walk to the new school.

A local census showed that Kennett's school population was growing rapidly. In the last weeks at the old school in the spring of 1906, there were 169 pupils and only one teacher. Three teachers were hired for the fall of 1906. When the school opened in September of 1906, eighty pupils showed up the first day, and 120 were registered by October 5, 1906. Miss Elizabeth Gregg was in charge of the first and second grades with forty-six students; Miss Etta M. Dennis had grades three, four, and five, with

AS AN INVESTMENT

BUTTERS'

Town Lots for Homes

are unequalled

At Kennett

No saloons. No Smoke. Plentiful supply pure uncontaminated water. Electric lights. Highest, healthiest part of Kennet. Adjoins smelter site. Postoffice and School adjacent. Drop a postal for further particulars.

S. M. STONE, Kennett

Courier Free Press, March 10, 1906

The Kennett School c. 1907–08. Lloyd Golinsky is standing fourth from left. (Courtesy of Golinsky family)

forty-three pupils; Miss Alice Smith, who was the principal, also taught grades six through nine. Among the pupils at various times during the next decade were three Golinsky first cousins, Lloyd Golinsky (Jake's son), Reta Golinsky (Charley's daughter), and Martha Gans (Hennie's daughter).

Strict discipline was enforced at the new school. The *Searchlight* reported on October 5, 1906, that "Miss Alice M. Smith, the principal … has the boys and girls trained like many miniature soldiers." When the bell rang, the children stopped playing and fell into their various lines, according to their grades, on each side of the main entrance. The smaller "baby" class was nearest the door, the older children, "patriarchs," behind.

When the command was given to march, a snare drum was beaten by Miss Smith to mark the time for the march. The paper reported that the pupils marched with military precision to their proper rooms, took their seats quietly, and began their work. The *Searchlight* (October 5, 1906) stated that "all is so quiet within the building that a person on the outside would hardly know that the school house contained a living soul." Pride in the new school was emphasized in various reports. There was pride in the newness, the neatness, and a great determination (apparently by military discipline if necessary) to keep it that way.

As the numbers of employees at the Mammoth Mine and Smelter grew, so did the families. It was the policy of the Mammoth Mine ownership to prefer their workers to be family men. To this end, they constructed small cabins and new cottages for workers and their families. In February 1906, another smaller school district was formed to take care of these children. By February 9, 1906, they had over twenty children and hired one teacher. By 1909, the population of Kennett reached 2,500 and another teacher was added.

Rosa Golinsky's offer to start a fund and donate a lot for a school and an ecumenical type house of worship had found no takers. Probably it was regarded as completely insane by other pillars of the community. In contrast to Rosa's offer, Mrs. Butters Sr., as reported, donated a lot for the new school and also donated over $1,700 for a fund to start building a Methodist church. This church was to be built on a lot donated by the Mammoth Company and located approximately two blocks from the new school.

In March of 1906, Ira Merrill, chairman of the church committee, started fund-raising for the new Methodist church. It was to be located in the new north upper section of Kennett, called the Smelter Addition which, despite its name, was considered by many to be the desirable new center of Kennett. The Methodist church was built using materials from the former church in Keswick.

On August 30, 1906, Bishop J. W. Hamilton of San Francisco came to Kennett to dedicate the new house of worship (*Free Press,* September 30, 1906). In September, the Reverend J. J. Pardee, a cousin of the governor of California, took over the new Methodist church. The congregation supplied a parsonage for him that was also built largely from material brought over from the demolished church in Keswick. This was not completed until March 1907, at which time it was occupied by Mr. and Mrs. Clarence Aldrich, the new minister and his wife.

In 1906, both the Catholics and Baptists started churches of their own. The Catholics drew a large part of their membership from the workers at the smelter, many of whom were from Italy and traditionally Catholic. The Mammoth Company, Charles Butters and Ira Merrill, were also busy building new, larger homes in this area.

Despite the rejection of her more idealistic schemes, Rosa Golinsky must have been considered a renowned social hostess, the Perle Mesta (a famous hostess in Washington, D.C., in the 1950s) of Kennett. She seemed to have been viewed as the proper person to undertake all semiofficial social duties that required education, flair, and presence. This is the most logical explanation for the article in the *Free Press* on March 3, 1910, which reported that Mr. and Mrs. Golinsky met train Number Fourteen from the south to greet Bishop Moorehouse, whose mission in Kennett was to baptize the large number of babies recently born there. No doubt this greeting of the bishop included a complimentary room at the Kennet Hotel, since train Number Fourteen was scheduled to arrive in Kennett at 1:45 A.M.

Chapter 11

Tram, Smelter, and Building Boom

The Mammoth Company was growing rapidly. In 1905 it had changed from mechanical roasters to blast furnaces, which were thought to be more efficient. The furnaces did smelt the ore very effectively, but led to large quantities of fumes sent out into the air. The company then installed bag houses, whose use was thought to filter out pollutants. The next step taken was to erect a tall smokestack similar to that built at Coram. Kennett's smokestack was 150 feet high and 12 feet in diameter (*Free Press,* April 9, 1906).

One other very visible sign of the new smelter structure was the building of an aerial tramway in 1905 to carry ore from the mine to the smelter 3,000 feet below. The construction made use of metal towers that fed steel cable to the lines holding ore buckets. The rate of delivery was planned to be fifty tons of ore an hour. The initial cost of the tramway system was estimated at $50,000. This was considered a bargain compared to the extremely expensive railroad that had been built by the Mountain Copper Company at Keswick.

The aerial tramway system was built by the Riblet Tramway Company, an engineering firm composed of three brothers. The president was B. C. Riblet, with offices in St. Louis, Missouri; the vice president was Royal N. Riblet of Spokane, Washington, and the third was W. S. Riblet, located in Nelson, British Columbia. The company run by these three brothers was known for its progressive and aggressive business methods. It devised, manufactured, and installed tramway systems all over the world in difficult types of terrain (*Free Press,* February 22, 1906). The Mammoth tramway that was designed and built by the Riblets was called "superhuman" (*Free Press,* February 22, 1906). Its line of travel, then called an "airline," was over notoriously precipitous terrain and wild scenery.

The brother overseeing the Mammoth construction, Royal N. Riblet, had his work cut out for him. He designed the project, ordered the necessary material, and oversaw the job. There were many hitches in the work. Poor grade ore used in the casting of the gripping machinery had to be replaced by heavier material, steel. In the fall of 1906 the tramway went into full operation. At this time, the cable lines needed tightening before the extra weight, added by the ore for the third furnace, would be thrown at it. This additional weight also caused changing the position of one of the steel towers. The remarkable equilibrium of the cable system caused much wonder. Only two buckets of ore were needed to start the upper cable line and only three to start the lower one. Royal Riblet was ready to leave Kennett, knowing that his tremendous engineering system was a complete success.

This may not have been the case with his personal life. During his stay in Kennett, he had met my mother, Miss Rubie Radzinski, and was attracted to her. They saw quite a lot of each other, riding horseback into the hills and taking other outings. Miss Rubie seems to have returned some of Mr. Riblet's feelings. How much, we can't know. Exactly what happened next is clouded. What we do know is that Royal N. Riblet left Kennett in October 1905, and by May 1906, Miss Rubie was back with her other family in Chicago. My mother, Rubie, never returned to Kennett, but spent the next few years with her uncle and family

Gravity road at the Mammoth Mine. (Special Collections, Meriam Library, California State University, Chico)

(her father's brother), in Chicago. In 1908 she met my father, Isadore Blumenthal, and they were married in February 1909.

Speculation as to the cause of the end of the romance with Mr. Riblet is all that is left to us. Maybe he changed his mind, not being ready to be serious. Maybe the Golinskys felt that however

Aerial tramway at the Mammoth Mine. (Special Collections, Meriam Library, California State University, Chico)

eminently qualified Mr. Riblet was, there was one drawback, he was not Jewish. Since the Golinskys seemed not to have paid any attention to Judaism, this is doubtful, yet it seems that when it comes to marriage this often makes a difference. And so, the Kennett chapter of my mother's life had come to a close. But, the saga of Kennett and of the Golinsky family went on.

The Golinskys were known by and large for their service to the community. For at least a decade, Bernhard had been selected by the board of supervisors to serve as an officer overseeing elections. He served as an election judge for the Bryan–McKinley election of 1900 and in many local and state elections. During 1907 political divisions grew sharply into political rivalries. Most of the older, established Kennett residents felt that there were enough regulations in place and opted for a more relaxed law enforcement policy. Generally, the Golinskys sided with this group, voting Democratic, although there was a growing diversity of opinion within the family. Jake, the youngest adult member of the family, had his independent ideas, and was elected as a Republican delegate to the Shasta County convention. Ben Jr. was a registered voter since 1909. He listed himself as a Progessive.

Kennett had always been a lively place politically. Many residents served on the Shasta County Board of Supervisors, and over the years a few went to the state legislature in Sacramento. As an indication of growth, the number of registered voters in the Kennett precinct tells the tale: In 1904 there were only 44 registered voters; in October 1906, there were 333. All were men, of course. Rosa, however, registered as a Democrat in 1911 when the state of California granted suffrage to its adult female residents (*Women of the West Museum of California,* 2003).

In 1907 a movement grew to apply for the incorporation of the town of Kennett. This status would force the town to adopt more stringent rules on many fronts. As a first move toward incorporation, the creation of a "pound district" was proposed. In such a district, all livestock had to be fenced in/out or tied up. Incredibly, up to this time, Kennett had been considered open range, and cattle, pigs, and other domestic livestock wandered freely through town. The surprising fact was that no wandering livestock had ever been hit by a train. A plan to establish a pound district was sent to the county board of supervisors, who promptly tabled it.

This pound issue had been backed by the same group of landowners and businessmen who were seeking incorporation. It was an indication of the growing power of this group that the political plum of postmaster, which had been in Golinsky family hands since inception, was taken away and awarded to a political rival, Alva Merrill (son of Ira), whose family was strongly allied with Charles Butters and his mostly Republican associates.

In the general election of November 1906 W. D. Tillotson, the prominent Shasta County attorney, had been elected district attorney. His opponent, Charles H. Braynard, challenged the results and requested a recount. A recount was undertaken in February 1907, and Tillotson still came out ahead, but by a very small margin. Mr. Tillotson soon was known to all by his zeal in enforcing laws, especially those dealing with gambling. This was not universally appreciated. The *Free Press* headline of January 15, 1907, read, LID SCREWED ON TIGHT IN KENNETT. W. D. Tillotson had ordered that every gambling game be closed at once. The constable, Tim Foley, had the unenviable job of making the rounds to all establishments, notifying them that gambling must stop.

News of the developing copper boom had reached the outside world. People in great numbers were coming to Kennett. There was still a chronic shortage of housing; no matter how fast houses went up, population outstripped the supply. A new housing community, soon called Little Italy, sprang up near the smelter. It was also less kindly called Dago Town, due to the large number of workers of Italian ancestry (Jones, 1985). Many workers lived in the small houses built by the Mammoth Company. These were considered by many residents to be an improvement over housing that they had experienced in other mining towns.

There was very little mixing of workers who lived in Little Italy and the more prosperous group of engineers, managers, and store and saloon owners. These wealthier citizens of Kennett built their homes up the hill, fulfilling Charles Butters' dream of an elegant uptown. Some of these homes were quite large, Victorian-style dwellings with extensive and colorful flower gardens. At this time, the township of Bernhard was platted, as was the West Kennett Addition, both owned by Bernhard Golinsky. He intended these areas to be moderate in price and for workers and their families.

It was not long before Kennett developed into a town with a major two-class social system. There was a third class, so far down the social hierarchy that it was almost never mentioned; this class was made up of the Native Americans and any Asian immigrants who had escaped the Chinese Exclusion Riots. Although the children from Little Italy went to the Kennett School, they walked to and from their separate residential areas and did not mix with other children. As it grew, Little Italy developed its own stores, saloons, gambling dens and a banking system headed by Antonio Carattini, one of the most influential members of this

Area called Little Italy located "conveniently" near the smelter. (Special Collections, Meriam Library, California State University, Chico)

community. He became its banker and owner of much property including the Mount Shasta Hotel, which was located at the point where the road began its climb to the Mammoth Mine. Mr. Carattini died in 1918 of Spanish influenza, leaving a son and his wife, Madelina.

Mrs. Carattini possessed a good business sense, plenty of money, and a dynamic personality. She took over the family's business interests. For a time, she managed the Kennet (Golinsky's) Hotel. She and Rosa Golinsky became wary partners and competitors in business ventures that were full of conflicts. Mrs. Carattini started buying many houses in Kennett despite the growing rumors that Kennett was a possible site for a large dam.

In 1907, the Mammoth Smelter became the largest operation in Shasta County, overtaking the Balaklala at Coram. Kennett was incorporated in 1911, at which time it became the second largest city in Shasta County, after Redding, and overtaking Keswick. At this time, the population of Kennett was estimated to be around 3,000 (*The Covered Wagon,* 1967, p. 12). During this period, railroad shipments of the smelted products were thought to be worth at least $20,000 a day. This made Kennett the largest and busiest shipment station between Sacramento and Portland, Oregon (Dittmar, *Copper Outlook,* 1913).

January and February of 1907 was a period of storms and devastating floods. The dirt roads of Kennett turned into a gooey sludge, and for weeks they were impassable. Several horse and wagon teams became hopelessly mired in the mud, and the four-horse team of B. C. and J. Golinsky tipped over at the Mammoth Grade. All contents of the wagon were lost in the mud, but fortunately the horses and the driver escaped injury. The Sacramento River rose rapidly (ten feet in two days), as did the Pit and the McCloud. A ferry, taking Greek immigrant workers to Ingot, capsized, and eleven men did not have the same luck as the horses and were drowned.

High water subsided by the end of March. As the water

receded, the damage was revealed to be greater than was first thought (*Free Press,* March 22, 1907). Piles of lumber that had been stacked up at building sites had been washed away, including lumber being used to build the new Kennett (Golinsky) Hotel. J. S. Smithson, one of Kennett's older residents, lost a warehouse and its contents. He said he never remembered so much water in Kennett. Considerable damage was done to the rear of those buildings located on the south side of Railroad Avenue, and many storage rooms and their contents were washed away. The new bridge across Backbone Creek, built by A. R. Myers, although built four feet higher than specified, still flooded and would have to be repaired. It was thought to be remarkable that it had stayed in place at all. The overflowing of Backbone Creek swept away a pile of lumber meant for the extension of the Holt and Gregg road to the Golinsky Mine. And, a hundred tons of hay was ruined when the floodwaters invaded the recently constructed Golinsky warehouse near the depot. Probably the most dramatic event occurred in the red-light district, where a whole twelve-room building and its contents, though presumably not its residents, floated away, heading rapidly down river, looking like a large river boat.

The vile weather of January, February, and March 1907 slowed the pace of new building in Kennett, but it did not stop it entirely. Building lots were selling well in various subdivisions platted and owned by Charles Butters. Lots in the new town of Bernhard also were selling. Many workers in Kennett reinvested their money in the future town. Optimism about Kennett was at an all-time high.

Possibly the largest, single construction in Kennett in 1907 was the building by the Golinsky family of the new Kennet Hotel. Although scheduled to open on the Fourth of July, it was delayed by the bad weather and loss of lumber in the floods. New lumber arrived in May, and a frantic building program began. The new hotel was located on the site of Kennett's first and only

The new Kennett (Golinsky) Hotel. (Courtesy Golinsky family and Shasta Historical Society)

building, Ollie Whitten's old store and rooming house. In addition to this site, the new hotel spread westward over several other lots now owned by the Golinsky family.

The new hotel was three stories high, had three porches which were each seventy-five feet wide across the southern front side of the building, and had a large and comfortable lobby and an enlarged dining room. There were 100 sleeping rooms, and every room was wired for electricity. The *Free Press* described the hotel in a positive light, stating on June 3, 1907, "The very best sanitary plumbing is being done throughout the building." The hotel did manage to open by July Fourth of 1907, even though most of the sleeping rooms were unfurnished. The public was invited for a free drink at the redecorated bar, an invitation responded to in a hearty manner. The April 30, 1907, edition of the *Copper Outlook* had described the hotel as "one hundred rooms, fresh … pure

Fourth of July parade, 1907 (Courtesy Balma family)

water ... sanitary ... old patrons still remember the Golinsky table and kind treatment ... new dining room decorated under the supervision of Mrs. Golinsky...."

The town's celebration of this Fourth in town was considered a great success, especially when compared to the previous Fourth in 1906 when the holiday had been ignored. In 1906 it had been just another workday because the Mammoth Mine and Smelter not only did not close down, but operated at full speed. The *Free Press* described the celebration in 1907 stating:

> Kennett's great Fourth of July celebration will go down in the history of the place as one of the biggest and grandest public demonstrations ever held in a smelter town. (*Free Press,* July 5, 1907)

The town was crowded. The parade began at ten o'clock in the morning, and contained decorated floats of the youngest young ladies, as well as floats for the Goddesses of Liberty and the State of California. Carriages carried the scheduled speakers. There was even a float for the Fraternal Order of The Red Men, who appeared dressed as Native Americans. In all likelihood, these "Indians" were the only Native Americans present at this celebration of liberty.

Chapter 12

Modern Kennett

In May 1905 Kennett's first newspaper, the *Copper Outlook*, was published. It was scheduled to appear weekly, and the first printing of one thousand copies sold out within a few hours. The publisher was H. O. F. Dittmar, who operated out of an office on Railroad Avenue. Each issue covered mining news, the train schedule, political announcements, a list of guests registered at the Kennett hotels, as well as local events of interest and business advertisements. It was published until around 1915. Only a few single copies of this paper have been preserved. A complete file would have revealed many otherwise unavailable items about Kennett.

A second paper, the *Kennett View,* began publication in 1906. It seems to have been issued for about three years. The publisher was Warren D. Pratt, referred to in the Redding *Courier Free Press* on July 16, 1908, as "the William Randolph Hearst of Kennett." In January 1907 he sold the paper to someone from Salt Lake City. In June of 1909, the *Courier Free Press* announced Mr. Pratt's retirement from active management of his paper and reported that he had leased his plant to H. E. Bedford. There is no evidence that Mr. Bedford was the man from Salt Lake City. In any event, nothing was done with the *Kennett View*. Mr. W. D. Pratt meanwhile settled "up-canyon," and announced plans to visit the Alaska-Yukon-Pacific Exposition in Seattle. No copies of the *Kennett View* after this time are to be found.

A third paper, the *Kennett Itemizer,* made its appearance in 1909. It was published by Charles B. Hodgkin. A special edition was published on August 2, 1909, to celebrate Kennett's victory over Dunsmuir on the baseball diamond. One copy of this paper is preserved in the California State Library in Sacramento. In 1909 Kennett had these three newspapers, and in August they were joined by a fourth called the *Colonia Italiana.* This paper was owned and edited by L. Ferrari. The paper was entirely in Italian and was the first newspaper of its kind in northern California. Mrs. B. Golinsky, it was noted in the press, gave a banquet to honor members of the Kennett press corps (*Free Press,* August 8, 1909). Invited were the personnel of the *Copper Outlook,* the *Kennett View,* the *Kennett Itemizer,* and the new *Colonia Italiana.* She also invited newsmen from Redding, notably from *The Searchlight* and the *Courier Free Press.*

Almost all news about life in Kennett beginning around 1890 was reported in the Redding *Free Press,* a daily newspaper, which had a section of news from Kennett in every edition (see references for the various names used by this paper over the years). By the time of the Kennett fire of 1904 the *Free Press* had a local correspondent in Kennett who operated from a room in the Kennet Hotel.

In the rebuilding that took place in the aftermath of the great fire of 1904, many amenities made their appearance in Kennett. Among these was that by 1905, almost all buildings in Kennett had electricity. The Northern California Power Company had extended its lines from the Balaklala Mine at Coram, a distance of four and one half miles, to the new Mammoth substation at Kennett. From here one line extended to the Mammoth Smelter and Mine. Another line ran to the new town site of Bernhard. A third line ran into Kennett proper.

By January 1905 the newly remodeled and enlarged Kennet Hotel had electricity in every room. On January 13, 1905, the lights were turned on in Kennett. This event was duly celebrated that very night at the Kennet Hotel and Bar, a very popular hostelry. That day, as if to emphasize that all had not changed, a very large panther had been shot near Squaw Creek. The panther shooting was part of the lively discussion that night at the Kennett Hotel's bar, where the Golinskys had set up free drinks for all. The only damage done by the large, raucous crowd was the breaking of a large glass panel in the entry door to the bar. The landlord is reported to have taken this in good humor.

The power and properties of electricity were not fully understood when it was first installed. This was illustrated by the story of Grant Snyder, the superintendent of the Balaklala Mine. He took hold of a live electric wire carrying two thousand volts that lay across the entrance to the mine. Fortunately, Mr. Snyder was wearing rubber gloves and boots at the time. He was shocked, but not electrocuted (*Free Press,* March 18, 1904).

Following rapidly on the heels of electrification came the telephone. Its growth was slower than electric lights, as telephone service was expensive. Also, there were not many places to call. However, by June 12, 1905, there were fifteen telephones in Kennett "in working order" (*Free Press,* June 12, 1905). Among those connected were the hospital, B. and J. Golinsky (the store), and the *Copper Outlook*.

By October of 1905 there were thirty phones listed in Kennett Central. The subscribers were listed in the *Free Press* as:

> Mammoth Mine, Mammoth Smelter Office, Mammoth Company's hospital, Golinsky Company, Kennet Hotel, Kennett depot, Shasta House, Holt & Gregg, Bicksford's meat market, Hoff Brothers, The Owl, Peter Monga, Ray Joy, May Cantrell, Peter Ramsey, Lee Coarts, Carlson & Murphy, J. S. Smithson, Judge W. R. Conant, V. Warrens, Trinity Copper Company, Byrne & Kely, J. B. Lindsay, Wilcox livery stable,

Wilcox residence, Josepa Bordes' laundry, Dr. C. J. Teas, William Trewartha, Charles Butter's office.

The *Free Press* on March 20, 1906, provided an interesting report on the status of fresh dairy products. Due to the denuded landscape and growing air pollution, the area directly around the Mammoth Smelter was an unfit place for a dairy. Milk and cream had to be brought into Kennett from other areas of the county and, when it arrived, it was seldom very fresh. By March of 1906, with the growth of the smelter, there were already more than a 1,000 new residents living in the area around the Mammoth

The Mammoth Hospital, built for employees of the Mammoth Company but also used for Kennett residents. Located at the northern edge of Bernhard. Note the privy in left corner of building. (Special Collections, Meriam Library, California State University, Chico)

Smelter. There was no suitable location on the Kennett side of the Sacramento River to house and feed milk cows and to grow the hay to feed them.

This need was seen as an opportunity by C. A. Baust, a blacksmith at the Mammoth Smelter (*Free Press,* March 3, 1907). He purchased a 20-acre placer claim on the east side of the Sacramento River about three miles above Kennett. He named this plot Stillwater Farm. Here, Mr. Baust accumulated a herd of dairy cows and began a successful and much appreciated dairy business.

During most of the early years of Kennett there seems to have been a doctor in town, but serious cases were taken to Redding. When Fritz Weischmann was hit by a train in 1899, he was attended by a Dr. Fraser who seemed to have been in Kennett for several years. In 1905, and for many years thereafter, Dr. H. W. Heyford had his house and office on Railroad Avenue. The hospital constructed by the Mammoth Company was intended to serve employees at the mine and smelter, but it accepted other patients from Kennett. The chief physician at the hospital from 1908 to 1916 was Dr. J. P. Sandholt, who married the hospital nurse, Miss Kathleen Ross. Other doctors established by 1908 were Dr. G. J. Teas and his family, Dr. J. T. Edgecomb, and Dr. James T. Affleck, who came from Bodie, Mono County, California. He settled in a house on Lawson Street. When the Mammoth Company closed its hospital in 1919, a group of local doctors rented the first floor of the old Kennet Hotel and used it as a hospital.

In the 1880s, Ollie Whitten's rooming house, which became the Golinsky store and hotel, had carried simple medicines among its goods. Many of these items we would call patent medicines. After the 1904 fire, a real drug store, the Powell and Purkitt Drugstore, prospered. In August of 1906 William Trewartha bought out this store and moved the business to his new store and a residence across Lawson Street. His business was profitable enough that he purchased a new home in the Merrill

Addition to Kennett (*Free Press,* September 2, 1906). One of his most popular features was an ice cream parlor introduced that same summer, 1906.

From its very inception Kennett had a post office. As noted previously, the early post offices were located in the Golinsky store and the first postmaster was Charles Golinsky, succeeded by his uncle, Bernhard. In December of 1906, the Kennett Post Office had its own building and was made a third class post office with an attendant raise in salary for the postmaster. The volume of business handled by the Kennett Post Office was second only, in Shasta County, to Redding. When the class of post office was raised, the salary of the postmaster was raised to $1,400 a year. It was assumed that Charles Golinsky would be reappointed to receive the new salary. However, this princely sum now made the office a worthwhile plum. The *Free Press* noted on December 27, 1906, "the Republican politicians may conspire to deliver the place to one of the wheelhorses of the party."

This indeed was what happened. In February 1907, Alva Merrill, the druggist, was appointed postmaster. Alva was the son of Ira Merrill, a partner of Charles Butters. Alva's appointment was the first non-Golinsky postmaster in the history of Kennett. This was widely considered an insult to the "founding family." Following his appointment, Alva sold his drug store. He rented a room for the post office in the Butters brick building on Railroad Avenue; the building was considered safe and fireproof. As post-master, Alva became a well-known local figure and was called "Al" by most of Kennett. There is no record of what he was called by the Golinsky family.

On February 13, 1907, the *Free Press* ran a picture of the Golinsky family as they had looked when they had first arrived in Kennett. The picture was accompanied by a verse composed for the occasion by Rosa Golinsky entitled, "Kennett Twenty Years Ago," celebrating their arrival in Kennett in 1887. The reference to "our friend Lyons" refers to Frederick Lyons, general manager of the Mammoth Mine and Smelter. He was greatly admired by Rosa.

Apparently Rosa was in a poetic and musical mode. Already well known and locally famous for her cooking, poetry, and painting, in July of 1907 she added songwriting to her list of accomplishments. A song by her entitled, "If I Had Only Known" was published by Groom Music Company of Chicago (*The Searchlight,* July 11, 1907). A second song, "The Bride of the Blossom Field" was in progress, ready to be sent to the same publisher.

With summer coming, Kennett transformed into a makeshift summer resort. It did a credible job for a "smelter town." Friends and relatives came up from the San Francisco Bay Area for the nice weather. Fumes from the smelter did not seem to act as a deterrent. Among those arriving was Hennie's daughter, Martha, named in memory of Hennie's deceased sister. She was a close friend of her first cousin, Charley's daughter, Reta Golinsky. Jake's son, Lloyd, joined the girls in their fun. The woods and stream behind the Kennet Hotel became their playground. They had sweet treats from Trewartha's new ice cream parlor that opened in the summer of 1906.

In March 1907, the ore that was found at the Golinsky Mine was assayed to be higher in gold content than other copper ore samples (*Searchlight,* March 13, 1907). Employed at the mine were thirty men and there were plans for increasing to 100, although where they would have been placed is a mystery. In 1907 the Golinskys incorporated as the Golinsky Mining Company to start extracting gold. Bernhard was president and Jacob ("Jake") became the secretary. Charles ("Charley") was part owner. A property receiving as much publicity as the Golinsky Mine was bound to attract claimants. Around 1907, a man named Gross began a suit against the Golinskys, claiming the boundary line of the mine was on his property.

Reta and Lloyd Golinsky (first cousins) play dress-up in back of the hotel. (Courtesy Golinsky family)

The case was heard by Judge Head, with the dispute focusing on the rightful location of the north line between Section 33 and Section 28 on the Golinsky Mine property. The court decided that the line established by the surveyor, Charles Dozier, hired by the defendants, was a correct one. The case then went on to the Court of Appeals. Here Judge Head was upheld and his decision then became the basis for a plea to the Supreme Court. This court denied the plea and the case finally was ended. Lawyers for the defendant were W. D. Tillotson and James Isaacs. The relationship of the Golinsky's with Mr. Tillotson was drawing even closer. On January 29, 1907, the following headline in the *Courier Free Press* announced the decision, a victory for the Golinskys: SUPREME COURT UPHOLDS GOLINSKY TITLE. The article called this a "noteworthy decision in the case of *Gross v. Golinsky,* line of the famous property now clearly defined."

The changes in mine management and the growing role of W. D. Tillotson reflected his interest in this thriving property. On Bernhard's side, it showed his growing need for more help as well as an investment of capital. The nephews were growing away from Kennett in the direction of San Francisco, and Bernhard was growing old. He was almost seventy years old at the time of the Gross trial.

All these factors led to a big change in ownership and management. In November 1911, the Golinsky Corporation sold all of its mining claims and improvements at the Golinsky Mines to W. D. Tillotson. On the same day, Mr. Tillotson resold it back to the Golinsky Copper Company, creating an entirely new entity. This new company, the Golinsky Copper Company, remained the controlling arm of the Golinsky Group for the remainder of its existence (Book of Deeds, Shasta County Recorder, vol. 3, p. 483 ff, 1911). The larger percentages of the gold and silver contained in the Golinsky ore caused both great anticipation and frustration. It will be recalled that all ore mined in this region was difficult to smelt, referred to as "rebellious ores" in 1893 by Colonel Lyons (*Free Press,* January 18, 1893).

The reverse side of this prosperity was what one would expect. Despite precautions taken, polluted air was flowing down the Sacramento River canyon. With the blowing of the third furnace in March 1906, the amount of sulfur in the air was noticeable and mentioned in the Redding *Free Press* (*Free Press,* September 18, 1906). The Western Union Company noticed the rapidity with which its wires deteriorated as they went up the canyon (Signor, 1982, p.31). However, it was workers at the smelter who received the worst effects of the roasting process. The sulfur that was killing the surrounding vegetation marked these workers with green hair and whiskers.

Chapter 13

Vice, Crime, and Disasters

When land for the Methodist Church was donated by the Mammoth Company, there was a proviso that no liquor could be sold or given away on the grounds. This no liquor law created a small, dry island in a sea of alcohol that existed in the rest of Kennett. In addition to about twenty saloons already doing business, five more licenses for saloons were granted in the month of October 1906 alone. Every man had his favorite watering place, but the most popular and also the most famous was Slim Warrens' Diamond Bar.

The bars and saloons usually held another, and generally illegal activity, gambling. This was partially hidden from public view in the back rooms. Some citizens felt it their duty to take action against gambling. One such person was J. J. Schultz who, in April 1906, swore a complaint against a C. W. Payne for dealing a faro game at the Riverside Saloon. Payne fled and was not heard from again. Many people felt that this episode was but the first in a series of moves to tighten up Kennett. This was a big order, as it seems that every type of con game known to man visited Kennett. The *Free Press* wrote about this on May 5, 1906, in an article titled FLOATERS, MOVE ON!

> … some of the floating population of Kennett was told to float on by the officers Tuesday night. About the ninth of every month tinhorns, street fakers, and the like come to Kennett to spend the tenth, or pay day, but they are always ordered to move on and they do so in preference to spending the night in the Kennett jail.

The phrase "screwing the lid on Kennett" came to be used with increasing regularity. (*Free Press,* January 15 1907)

The third type of diversion was, of course, the red-light district. A red light was a signal clearly understood to be the location of a "house" of prostitution. This was dramatically illustrated by the two experiences related by my mother. She said,

> I had a friend named Mabel from Weed, who came to visit Kennett with her father. They stayed at the Kennet Hotel and while her father attended to business or entertained himself in some adult way, Mabel and I had the run of the house.
>
> One evening, while telling ghost stories, we darkened the room a bit by putting cloths or scarves over some of the lamps, which were kerosene. The lamp nearest the window we covered with a red scarf. It was not long before there came a series of knocks at the door and we heard men's voices asking to be let in. We were terrified.
>
> The unusual noise for this part of town soon drew Aunt Rosa's attention. She came storming in, shooed the men away, and noting the red scarf on the lamp, whipped it off. She gave us a terrible scolding. Neither Mabel nor I knew what we had done wrong, although the thought that the lamp might have caught fire did occur to us. …

That these two girls were as naïve as my mother made them out to be is believable given the way that girls of "gentle birth" were raised in those days. My mother had been orphaned at an early age and had no mother to tell her the facts of life. What really is incredible is that the same or a very similar story is told about Jake Golinsky's bride, Flora. In 1898, she was given an oil lamp with a red glass shade as a wedding present. As soon as she set up housekeeping in her new house in Keswick, she lit the lamp and set it in the window with predictable results.

Although it was now widely understood that the Golinsky's home was not "a house," those establishments that were houses became well known. There were at least seven or eight popular houses of prostitution, as well as numerous individual prostitutes who plied their trade from rented rooms (Balma, 1992). Law officers and upstanding citizens considered liquor, gambling, and prostitution necessary outlets for working men. Thus, they tolerated them as long as things were kept within bounds.

This pattern seems to have existed in all towns on the frontier and Kennett was no exception. What was so interesting was that the residents of the "good side" of town, the Golinskys, the Smithsons, the Butters, and the Lyons, among others, all succeeded in coexisting with this other world that was only a short walk from their homes.

While the reports of the new mines, the new stores, and the new hotel and places of entertainment seemed to paint a rosy picture of civilization in Kennett, the seamy, darker, criminal underside of the "real West" was just as active. Before the railroad was established, holdups and robberies of various sorts were frequent. The advent of the train posed a greater challenge, but seemed not to have discouraged the holdup men.

Around 1883, reports abounded of the holdup of the Butte Coach, a stagecoach robbery just out of Redding (*Free Press,* June 1883). In 1881, a sixteen-year-old boy and an adult companion held up the Weaverville-Redding stage. The boy eventually revealed where the guns and loot were hidden, in 1892. A "desperado highway man" (*Republican Free Press,* June 25, 1892) named John Ruggles, known to have shot and killed any who crossed his path, including Sheriff Buck Montgomery, was captured and brought by train to Redding for trial. The jail in Redding already held his younger brother, Charley. As the Redding *Free Press* of July 30, 1892, reported, "Fearful of the law's delays and inefficiency, the citizens usurped its authority, and local hero Buck Montgomery was avenged. Expensive trials were saved … ." In plain language, the Ruggles brothers were lynched.

On April 6, 1895, two men held up the Overland Express at Wheatland. This resulted in the death of one of the holdup men and of the sheriff of Tehama County. The robbers had climbed to the top of the coal tender, ordered the engineer to stop the train, and forced another trainmen to open the express car. The robbers made a sack out of a pant leg tied at the bottom and forced the engineer to hold this sack while passengers put their money and jewels into it. When they proceeded to the sleeping car, the sheriff woke up and was shot to death.

In October 1897, a highwayman held up the Yreka and Fort Jones Stage. He was captured after a gunfight at Delta, which then resulted in his death and that of one of his cronies. The description of this event in the Redding *Free Press* was detailed enough to have been used without many adjustments as a shooting script for a 1930's Hollywood cowboy movie.

The next year, an extraordinary theft of $1,200 in gold from one individual was perpetrated on the southbound overland train between Sisson and Dunsmuir. The victim had just returned from Dawson City, Yukon Territory, traveling from Seattle to San Francisco at the time of the robbery. These incidents are just samples of the events in the area. Several violent crimes were reported each week. In addition to holdups, men met death on runaway ore trains, falling between cars while switching, and suffered other train related accidents.

The trains themselves could not seem to avoid accidents. The new, powerful engines of the Southern Pacific were creating so much exhaust that they caused rocks to fall out of the roofs of tunnels. As early as December 1884 a train up from Redding to Delta was proceeding slowly due to slides and washouts, but not slowly enough to prevent the engine running off the track. The train had just emerged from Tunnel Number Four when it ran into a mass of rock and earth, throwing the engine off the track. Luckily, it was right side up and the coaches remained on the rails. The wrecking train came up the next day and cleared up the mess.

On October 8, 1887, two engines collided. One trainman died and several were injured. Two days later a brakeman was thrown off and killed as he tried to brake a runaway car. Similar accidents were reported in the newspapers on a nearly-weekly basis.

Additionally, accidents occurred due to other factors. The Redding *Free Press* related on October 12, 1898, "The locomotive of the 'swing' freight train jumped the track on an open switch at Kennett Wednesday." The following January, the southbound Overland hit a landslide just above Redding. Fortunately, it had been running slowly at the time, but the tender was thrown off the track and steps were torn off the first few cars.

On April 25, 1899, a really dramatic rescue occurred. A special train carrying the drama troupe known as The Bostonians was approaching Kennett from the south when Charles Schoonover, who worked for Bernhard Golinsky, was enjoying a walk. He noticed pieces of firewood about two feet long had been tied down to the rails on each side of the track. Mr. Schoonover realized that this would derail the train. He quickly removed the obstructions and less than twenty minutes later the special train that was moving at an extra fast speed came thundering by. The passengers and crew were utterly oblivious to the awful derailment they had been spared. It was never established who had tried to wreck the train.

In January 1900 rains had softened the soil to such an extent that a landslide occurred near Tunnel Number One, just below

Kennett. The train was held at Kennett while a crew came by special train from Redding and loaded the dirt on flatcars to be hauled out of the way. In May of the same year a freight train was wrecked by a slide at the same gap near Tunnel Number One. The engine and four cars left the track. The northbound passenger trains were held at Redding while this was cleared up.

In July of the same year, the California Express was racing along when the rear coach, a Pullman, left the track and pitched down a 60-foot embankment. It was saved from going into the river by a large boulder. The spot where this accident occurred had just been cleaned up from a previous freight train wreck. A temporary track had been installed, but could not take the speed of the racing Pullman. No passengers were killed, but it is thought that all were injured.

In October 1900, floods damaged the railroad tracks and caused several slides. In Keswick, the streets literally ran with water. A landslide at Keswick was cleared speedily by a crew rushed down from Kennett. After the northbound train passed, another slide occurred and was removed just in time for the train from the north. The following July, two passenger trains crashed head-on near Sisson at Black Butte summit. Two people were killed and 100 injured. Two locomotives were demolished as well as the mail car. The wreck was considered the worst of its kind on the Shasta route, and officials were thankful that it had occurred at this relatively straight and open spot. Had it occurred further south in the Sacramento River canyon, it was thought, there could have been many more fatalities.

Daily life as well seemed to have held an extreme number of tragedies for the inhabitants of the area. Quite a few of these were related to bad weather such as floods and very heavy snow causing deaths by drowning or from being crushed in collapsing buildings. The irony is, of course, that California always has used its wonderful climate as part of its boosterism. The tourist brochures rarely mentioned temperamental northern California weather.

Many accidents occurred at the mines. Safety regulations seemed to have been nonexistent. Shortly after the Uncle Sam Mine reopened in January 1900, part of it collapsed. A great tragedy was averted because the collapse occurred during the lunch hour; otherwise many would have been killed. The collapse was blamed on the heavy rains of the winter, which had softened the ground and made the mine tunnels wetter than usual.

Reports of accidents were described in what might seem to us as gruesome detail. In describing a man who met his death and was mangled by an ore car, the report described the "fingers and bits of flesh scattered for a hundred yards" (*Free Press,* 1905). Victims of death by burning were frequently described as "burnt to a crisp" (*Free Press,* 1905).

These were headlines about the area that were published in the Redding *Free Press* throughout the year of 1905:

> Man Fights for Life with a Bear ... Robbers Hold Up Red Bluff Salon ... Masked Robber Holds Up Keswick Saloon ... Man Fatally Hurt in Smelter Explosion ... Seriously Injured by Breaking Bicycle ... Train Held Up Near Eugene, Oregon ... Attacked Son with Post Hole Digger ... Caught on Pulley and Dashed to Death ... Many Are Killed in Train Wrecks ... Caught in Act of Robbing Wells Fargo Office ... Children Find Body of Ben Russell ... Gail Johnson of Kennett Killed By Mexican Peon ... Son Saw Father Crushed to Death ... Narrowly Escaped Being Cut in Two on a Pile Driver ... Yosemite Stage Held Up ... Chopped to Death with a Cleaver. ...

What is to be made of such a recital? The plain fact is that most of the residents of Kennett and the surrounding areas were hard working, honest, and somehow untouched by the mayhem happening in the neighborhood.

Although optimism and prosperity continued to grow during the early 1900s, nature stepped in, abetted by human error, with severe displays of power that tempered the optimistic mood. In February 1904, Shasta County received fifty-five inches of rain, causing many washed out homes and buildings. Hardest hit was Smithson's Hotel. Its yard was washed out above Backbone Creek. Damage would have been infinitely worse had not a dam, previously constructed by Charles Butters to bring good drinking water to Kennett, acted as a flood control device. The dam was a semicircular cement structure, eighty-five feet long, located about eight miles above Kennett. It had been finished in August 1903, about nine months before the devastating flood. Because of the vast amount of new buildings the damage caused by the floods was much more widespread.

A little after five o'clock on the morning of Wednesday, April 18, 1906, San Francisco was hit by a devastating earthquake. The quake itself and the extensive dynamiting that was used to stop the spread of fires caused at least five hundred deaths (*World Almanac,* 1950). The tremor was felt for miles around, including most areas of Shasta County. It was widely noted in Redding, Kennett, Keswick, and Sisson. In San Francisco martial law was proclaimed and the state militia was called in to patrol the city to prevent looting and to aid the stricken and homeless people. People without official business were prevented from entering the city.

Many families in Shasta County, as elsewhere in the state, had friends and relatives in San Francisco. For days after the quake there was chaos and confusion in the city and no accurate information was available as to the extent of the damage and the names of those who had perished.

During this terrible time of waiting for news, Rosa called a Golinsky family meeting to discuss what the family in Kennett could do to find and aid members of the family in San Francisco. As my mother recalled:

> It was decided that a family delegation should be sent to find members of the family and bring them back to Kennett for the duration of the crisis. Jake pointed out that people without official business were not allowed in the city, but that he had a plan. He said that he could make armbands that would resemble those worn by the Red Cross and this would let him pass the armed guards and get into the city. Jake volunteered to go and asked me to go with him, which I agreed to with a great deal of both excitement and fear. … We took the train to Oakland, managed to get on a ferry to cross San Francisco Bay, and went into the stricken city. Our armbands were taken for the real thing and we searched for the family. I will never forget the terrible ruins. …

At the time of the quake Hennie Gans and her daughter, Martha, were living in a boarding house on O'Farrell Street. The house was badly shaken, but was not destroyed. A piece of chimney had fallen through the roof and onto Martha's vacant bed. Hennie left Martha with her landlady and walked miles through the ruined city to her place of employment at Samuel's Lace House (Corson, 1999; Redburn, 1999). Understandably, she was the only employee reporting for work that day and her appearance amazed the owner. Hennie stayed a few hours to help the owner pack his precious lace goods in boxes that were then put on a wagon to be taken to safety. The building was not considered safe at that time. The amazed and grateful owner told Hennie to take whatever lace she wanted for herself. But Hennie was too proud to do this and she left empty-handed. With her duty done for her employer, she walked back the many miles to the boarding house.

Back at home Hennie and Martha packed a small trunk with necessities and left to walk to the California Street home of Hennie's sister-in-law, Regina Isaacs. They dragged the trunk behind them for many blocks before it became too heavy for them. At Filmore Street, they left the trunk with a woman, a perfect stranger, who took care of it in her house. For the rest of her life, Martha could recall the screech of the trunk as she and her mother dragged it behind them.

Hennie and Martha found the Isaac's house unharmed, unlocked, and unoccupied. Extremely hungry, they foraged for something to eat, but all they could find was a bowl of prunes which they devoured. Surely this snack must have added to their misery later in the day as they trudged to Golden Gate Park seeking the food and shelter that had been set up there. At the park, they joined the thousands seeking safety and watched San Francisco burn.

When the fires were controlled a few days later, Hennie and Martha made their way back to Filmore Street where they retrieved their trunk in perfect condition. They then walked back to the Issac's house on California Street. This area was west of Van Ness Avenue and was not touched by the fires. It was a few days later that they were found there by Jake and Rubie and taken to Kennett. They soon were joined by Ray (Mrs. Charles) Golinsky and her daughter, Reta. Jake's mother-in-law, Mrs. Rich, also came up to Kennett. All in all, the family felt lucky to have everyone well housed, fed, and in good health. During the period of the rebuilding of San Francisco both Reta and Martha became students at the Kennett School.

Unfortunately the railroads continued having their habitual wrecks. A glance at the train timetable for June 22, 1907, showed eight trains a day stopping at Kennett. Four were from the south and four were from the north. In addition to these trains, there were many freight trains hauling ore from the local mines, as well as lumber and other types of freight. Train numbers eleven and twelve were called the Shasta Express, and fifteen and sixteen were the Oregon and California Express. The trains were heavily used by the military for troop movements, and northbound trains carried fruit, machinery, and cattle.

In February 1906, a landslide above Delta hit the southbound train killing two passengers and stopping all trains in both directions for more than two days. Hundreds of men were called out to shovel the mass of earth, rock, and mud. Rain falling on the already soaked ground kept the slide coming down faster than it could be cleared. After thirty hours of continuous labor, enough land was cleared to lay a temporary track around the rest of the slide. While this was happening, hundreds of passengers were detained at Redding and Red bluff, causing a boom for restaurants, hotels, stores, and saloons.

On July 6, 1907, a freight train rear-ended another freight stopped in the Kennett yards. The engineer of the second train was fired because he had come into the station at too high a speed. The front train was carrying steers and sixty were killed in the accident. Fifteen escaped alive and ran around Kennett for several days until rounded up (*Free Press,* July 7, 1907).

To help handle its numerous mishaps, the railroad created a special train called "The Wrecker." It carried a group of specially trained men and various types of equipment. On July 31, 1906, the Wrecker was in Coram clearing up a freight wreck. Lumber cars had derailed, taking an airborne ride into the Sacramento River. The Wrecker, then was called to Kennett to clean up after the "wreck of steers" (*Free Press,* July 31, 1906).

While in Kennett, the Wrecker cleaned up the wreck of a car on the Mammoth Mine spur. Once this task was completed, the Wrecker pulled into a sidetrack to make way for the morning express. However, the derailing switch malfunctioned and the Wrecker itself became a wreck. One crewman was killed in this accident and seven were badly injured. This Wrecker's wreck was the fourth accident in the Kennett yard within a month.

In August of 1906 a fire occurred in Tunnel Number Six (near Elmore), which destroyed the supporting timbers. This caused a large section of the tunnel to cave in. It was necessary to retimber the tunnel before the rocks and dirt could be removed. Northbound passenger trains were held in Kennett and southbound trains were held at Dunsmuir. This repair job delayed all trains on the line for four days.

In the meantime, a swing engine was derailed in the middle of the Backbone Creek Bridge near Kennett. The Dunsmuir Wrecker was sent for but could not come until Tunnel Number Six was repaired! This long delay caused a scarcity of fruits and vegetables at Kennett, but the greatest crisis was the nonarrival of steam beer from the Redding suppliers. By the second day after the accident, half of the saloons were out of steam beer and the lager was running low (*The Searchlight,* August 9, 1906). This was especially critical as Kennett had become a great railroad center, playing host to all the northbound passengers who had to spend two nights at Kennett hotels and eat at the local restaurants and drink at the Kennett bars.

On October 7, 1906, a freight train derailed and seven loaded lumber cars left the track at a point about eight miles above Kennett. This accident was the third blockade of the Shasta route in three days. This one caused a twelve-hour delay during which all northbound trains were held at Kennett.

The wreck pattern continued into 1907 and beyond. In May of 1907, there was a wreck near Copley (also called Motion). Many Kennett people were in the Copley wreck. Some of them walked home, but it was reported in family lore that the women remained on the train all night. Among these was Rosa Golinsky. When she was finally delivered to Kennett, she took to her bed, having been badly shaken up. Is it any wonder that the *Free Press* had a regular new column called "The Daily Wreck"?

Chapter 14

Prosperity and Its Perils, 1906–1912

During the years of 1906–1907, amidst the frantic activity taking place in and around Kennett, subtle changes were taking place within the Golinsky family and in its role in the community. The close relationship between Rosa and Bernhard and Jake and Flora had become even tighter. Rosa would sign her name and was addressed as "Ma G." This form of address reflected the acceptance of Jake as her "real" son.

The wives of Jake and Charley became close friends and made friends with other wives in the town. Flora (Mrs. Jake) and Ray (Mrs. Charles) were frequently mentioned in newspaper items when visiting with Kennett friends or traveling to nearby towns. "Going up the river" was a frequent short jaunt for them as well as for many other Kennett residents. Favorite destinations were Castella, Dunsmuir, and Shasta Springs. Judge Conant, justice of the peace, had a summer home "up-canyon," near Castella, a spot famed for its fine fishing. Kennett itself wasn't such a bad fishing hole, either. In July 1908, it was recorded that a three and one-half pound trout pulled a fisherman off some slippery rocks into the river at Kennett (Redding *Free Press,* July 21, 1908).

Charley's connection with Kennett grew increasingly sporadic as his interests in San Francisco grew. Jake remained a true citizen of Kennett for a longer time, although he too had thoughts of breaking away. Over the years, Jake had become the best-known family member in Kennett. He was active in politics, sports, and social functions. In 1908 the Kennett chapter of the Mammoth Aerie of Eagles was formed. In the opening ceremonies on February 24, 1908, Jake Golinsky was listed among the ninety-one members.

Jake still played left field on the Kennett baseball team called the Smelter City Nine. He was getting a little old for the sport and the Redding *Free Press* at times printed some "humorous" remarks about his performance. His fielding was described as "okay," but his batting was very weak. The Smelter City Nine played the Mammoth Mine employees, and Kennett won 16–13. On July Fourth of 1908 Jake's team won in tight games over Corning and Delamar.

A substantial indication of changes in the Golinsky family's relationship to Kennett occurred in July 1908 when Bernhard, Jake, and Charley Golinsky sold their well-established store to the Charles Baer and Clare Company. This store was the oldest business establishment in Kennett; it was the outgrowth of Charley Golinsky's original Kennett purchase from Ollie Whitten in 1885–1886. This sale of the Golinsky property was the outward manifestation of the changes going on within the group.

There were rumors around town to the effect that the family might move to the coast. It was surmised that they would keep their homes in Kennett, as they still owned mining interests "of great value" (*Free Press,* July 15, 1908). In July, Bernhard and Jake, with their wives, left for an extended visit to San Francisco. Charles remained in Kennett to oversee the family's mining interests. He was to be the contact for the American Smelting and Refining Company, which was leasing the Golinsky Mine.

Jake returned to Kennett in September 1908, declaring that Kennett still looked good to him. He had not found business interests in the Bay Area to suit him. When Mr. Clare of the Baer and Clare Company decided to sell out his interest in the recently purchased store, Jake bought up his partnership and once again became a Kennett merchant. The store was now called The Baer and Golinsky Store. New improvements were made, including a large plate glass window across the front. The groceries were separated from the dry goods to make a more "modern" store. In November of 1908 there was a string of robberies of businesses in town. The new Baer and Golinsky Store was one of the victims. Some cash was stolen, but no damage was done to the store (*Free Press,* December 2, 1908).

Rosa and Bernhard continued their travels that included a lengthy visit to Florida, as befitted people of substantial means. During their absence Kennett was again plagued by heavy winter storms. January 1909 saw heavy rainfall. In one day ten inches fell in twenty-four hours (*Free Press,* January 19, 1909). The barroom floor at the Kennet Hotel was covered with a foot of water. Rain changed to snow by the twenty-forth of January. The aerial tram at the Mammoth Mine began to sag. When the snow melted, it caused washouts and floods up and down the Sacramento Valley as far as Marysville. Kennett's precipitation for January 1909 was a record of fifty-four inches (*Free Press,* January 1909). Phone and electric lines were downed and services were disrupted. There was some speculation about the reason for the ferocity of the weather and the extent of the damage. A few timid souls hinted that there might be some reason found on the hillsides so badly denuded by the smelter fumes. This was an incredible thought and was not generally accepted at this time.

Rosa and Bernhard missed the fury of the storms. They returned home from Florida in March of 1909 and were welcomed with enthusiasm. The *Free Press* on March 8, 1909, welcomed them as "the Father and Mother of Kennett." During their absence, those left in charge of the hotel had allowed the service to slip. In the summer of 1909, Rosa and Bernhard closed the dining room to refurbish it and improve the cooking and service. It was reopened on August 10, 1909, and it was widely announced that the dining room would again be under the personal management of Mrs. B. Golinsky.

In 1909 a movie theatre was installed on the ground floor of the Kennet Hotel. The first show opened March 9, 1909. During this time, the rest of Kennett was perking up as well, with other new ventures opening. Mrs. Warren, Mrs. Trewartha, and Mrs. Endicott started a new public hall at Bush and Lawson Streets that brought a bar, for the first time, two blocks above Railroad Avenue. Henry Weinhardt of Portland, Oregon, built a bottling plant. His beer became a popular, well-known brand that is available to this day. In March of 1909, an ice factory and cold storage building were built adjoining it. Another cold storage facility was built next to the Baer and Golinsky warehouse near the railroad station. It was to hold bottled beers and mineral waters.

Two new social halls opened in 1909. One was at the Mammoth Mine where large dances and suppers were provided to all local residents. Another theatre and hall was opened by V. E. Warrens, D. Endicott, and W. Trewartha. For its opening, the ladies of the Catholic Church made box suppers which were sold for a total profit of $112 to benefit the church.

As mentioned earlier, around 1910 incorporation was a large issue occupying the minds of Kennett's citizens. Kennett was eligible for the status of a sixth class city, defined as having more than 300, though less than 3,000 individuals residing in its city limits. As a sixth class city, Kennett would have the advantages of collecting fees for liquor and other licenses within the city for local use. It soon became apparent that the issue was not whether to incorporate, but how much of Kennett should be included in the incorporation.

Three plans were in circulation. The first plan was called Lesser Kennett and included only the central business area and the residences that could be viewed from this area. The second plan called itself Greater Kennett, and included more homes uphill and all buildings down to Big Backbone Creek. The third plan might have been called the Greatest Kennett, and was inspired by M. E. Arrighini, the founder of Kennett's Italian-American newspaper. He called himself the oldest citizen of Kennett and his plan was to include Kennett proper, plus all new uphill development. Also included in this plan were the Mammoth Smelter property, the Holt and Gregg lime works, "Little Italy," and the Bernhard addition to Kennett.

All three plans were submitted to the county board of supervisors after more than a year of mass meetings and public debate. Initially, Mr. Butters was opposed to any incorporation, fearing higher taxation. At a mass meeting held on February 10, 1911, held at the opera house, over one hundred citizens voted in favor of incorporation with the Greatest Kennett plan. George W. Metcalfe, general manager of the Mammoth Copper Company, spoke on behalf of the company and graciously said that he would be satisfied with whatever the citizenry decided to do (*Free Press,* February 10, 1911). His company would not stand in the way of progress.

It was agreeable to the Mammoth Company that the Mammoth's residential district be included in the corporate limits. However, to avoid taxes, the Mammoth Smelter, mine, and offices were not to be included in the boundaries of the incorporation. It was pointed out that Kennett would receive all revenue derived from saloon and mercantile licenses, to be used to pay for better police, fire protection, and better streets and sidewalks. The city would not have to pay the county any road taxes, but would have to keep up is own "highways and biways [*sic*]" (*Free Press,* February 2, 1911).

Accordingly, an election for incorporation was set up. On April 1, 1911, Kennett became a city. The vote carried 205 for, 43 against (*Free Press,* headline: KENNETT IS NOW A CITY IN FACT, APRIL 1, 1911). The new city officers were as follows: Marshal, W. W. Middleton; clerk, S. E. Smithson; treasurer; Bernhard

Golinsky; and trustees, J. N. Gregg, W. P. Milburn, William Welsh, Victor E. Warrens, and E. Thompson. Bernhard's opponent was his post office rival, Alva Merrill, whom he beat 102 to 58. At the first meeting of the Kennett city officers, J. N. Gregg was elected mayor. The city board met almost every night for a week, setting up ordinances, salaries, and a fee scale for licenses.

The growth, civic pride, and enthusiasm of Kennett were based on the continuing operation and prosperity created by the Mammoth Mine and Smelter and the smattering of smaller operations such as the Golinsky Mine. The Mammoth Mine and Smelter, although creating a tremendous amount of employment, had its cost, both for the workers at the plant, and the other residents of the area. Working at the mine was both exhausting and hazardous. The mine itself was located at about 3,500 feet above the town. Many men stayed up at the mine on their days off because the climb down to town consisted of almost four miles of steep mountain to be followed by a climb back up twenty-four hours later (Jones, 1985).

Working conditions at the mine and smelter were unpleasant and hazardous. The smelter air contained lethal fumes. Many men were maimed, burned, or killed working in the open molten liquid vats, or near belts and cables. Men died from heat prostration. Accidents were frequent and considered routine news in the local papers. Despite the hazards, jobs at the mine were sought after. The work paid decently, was steady, and company and private housing was above average. By 1908 over 800 men were employed at the mine and smelter, and the payroll had reached a $1,000,000 per month. The company was producing about two-thirds the copper produced in California.

While mining was the most important industry in Shasta County, agriculture was growing increasingly important. In past years, most of the farms were small, single-family self-contained units. But these were rapidly being converted into single-fruit cash crop acreage. Citrus farms were becoming increasingly

Mammoth Smelter (Courtesy Balma family)

lucrative, and citrus farmers were more numerous, vocal, and powerful.

Smelter fumes heavily damaged the farmer's young fruit trees. As the farmers became increasingly concerned, they formed protective associations. Centered in the Anderson Valley was the

Mammoth Smelter (Courtesy Balma family)

Shasta County Farmers Protective Association. In 1908, this group hired T. W. Shanahan as its legal counsel. With his help they decided to attack the Balaklala Smelter at Coram and the Mammoth Smelter at Kennett. A decision in a similar suit in Utah that favored the farmers, and was decided by Judge Marshall of the U. S. Circuit Court, was the basis for the Shasta County suit. One provision of Judge Marshall's decision was that fumes released from the smelters could contain no more than three quarter of one percent of sulfur dioxide by volume.

The Mammoth Company was willing to go to great lengths to preserve its lucrative business. It was thoroughly familiar with the Utah decision. When faced with the suit, it immediately decided to take drastic measures to comply with the farmers' demands to cut down on pollution. The Mammoth Company's method was to install bag houses that were basically enormous vacuum cleaners, to clean the particulate pollutants out of the smoke and to release cleaner smoke into the air. The bag house had been used as a fume control device elsewhere, but previously had been used for zinc and lead, not copper. The bag house mixed smelter fumes with air by forcing fumes through fans and pipes. The remaining dust became a large disposal problem.

The bag house smokestacks and view of the smelter. (Courtesy California State University, Chico)

The structure built at the Mammoth for this operation was bigger than the smelter itself, and cost more than $250,000 to build. The company called on the bag house inventor, C. B. Sprague, to be consultant during construction. The huge smokestack was demolished. The farmer's association agreed not to pursue any suits and claims while the company was installing the smoke control device. Most of the same agreements were made with the Balaklala, which was trying a different device but eventually decided to close down its smelter.

In October of 1910, a delegation of farmers visited the Mammoth bag house. The size must have been overwhelming, but other conclusions were elusive. The local papers proclaimed the bag house a success. First reports were ecstatic; the *Free Press* on July 2, 1910, stated that it "works like a charm ... smelter smoke ancient history." In fact, a great deal of adjustment was needed as workmen were bothered by gas, haze, and smoke, and an unpleasant smell was noticeable all over Kennett. In 1912, grain farmers visited Kennett to make a formal complaint to the Mammoth Company management. They, however, were impressed by the extent of the improvements made in the bag house (*Free Press,* March 27, 1912).

In December 1910, encouraged by the perception, if not the actuality, of the efficiency of the bag house, the Mammoth Company blew its third furnace. Almost 3,000 men now worked at the company (Jones, 1985). Business was so good that a fourth blast furnace was under consideration. Hoping to overcome what the Mammoth Company felt was "bad press," a photographer was hired to take pictures of men working at the smelter, the nice little houses, and other positive aspects of the operation. However, it says a great deal about the mindset at the time that these photos also showed the landscape, denuded by smelter fumes, visible behind the buildings and this was not viewed by the management as "bad press." In December of 1910 the *Kennett*

View reported that new green buds and leaves were sprouting from shrubs on the mountainsides.

In some peculiar way, the town of Kennett itself seemed to have escaped the worst of the fumes. Perhaps this was simply the perception of its residents. This may explain the recollections of two of them. When asked what she remembered about living in Kennett in 1919, Mrs. Georgia Hanson promptly said, "the fruit, the wonderful fruit, especially the plums, but the blackberries and peaches were wonderful too" (Hanson, 1995). A similar response was given in an interview with Tog Balma in 1969. Mr. Balma recalled the wonderful peaches of his childhood. When questioned how this could be so, Mr. Balma offered the opinion that the fumes had killed the insects that would have harmed the trees (Montarbo, 1969)!

Frequent fires still plagued Kennett. In 1909 a fire board had been elected to handle the problem. Their first improvement was to move the fire hydrants and plugs away from the walls of buildings along Railroad Avenue. These were moved into the Southern Pacific reserve space where they could be reached easily. A new bronze fire bell was ordered, and the New Year's Eve dance netted $62.30 towards the bell (*Free Press,* January 1, 1909). Mrs. B. Golinsky donated twenty $20, which she had just received from the sale of her latest song, "Longing." In February 1910, a large new bronze bell arrived and was placed on a specially built fire tower just up Lawson Street from the railroad.

In March 1912, twenty businesses on Railroad Avenue and Lawson Street were burned in a raging fire that lasted just one hour. Among the losses were nine saloons, four lodging houses, two grocery stores, three restaurants, and two barbershops. The fire had started in the basement of the W. R. Conant Building. The firemen worked tirelessly, but saved only the huge Kennet Hotel and Baer's store. Victor Warren's asbestos curtain saved his Diamond Bar. James Smithson was burned out for the third time. This fire was considered to have been caused by arson.

In the 1910 census, of the members of the Golinsky family, only Rosa, Bernhard, and Ben Jr. were listed as living in Kennett. With all the other siblings gone to live in San Francisco, Ben Jr. now became his uncle's partner in business and various other ventures and activities. They were often joined by W. D. Tillotson. In one such venture, the three filed a claim on an oil well called the Flora V. It was located on 160 acres near Squaw Creek.

The new Kennett fire bell, 1912. (Courtesy of Shasta Historical Society)

Ben Jr. had lived in Kennett since 1890, but he was still the least known member of the family. This was partly due to his taciturn nature. He seemed to have avoided social contact outside the family, and he remained a lifelong bachelor. He certainly saw a great number of people, as he was the Kennett postmaster from 1893 until 1906. But, in this job he was separated from people by a counter and a cage.

Ben ran a small retail business and had his own little house built. During the prosperity after 1905, he built several other small cottages that he either sold or rented. His name appeared in the local papers only occasionally, and this usually was to report that the postmaster had taken a vacation. His favorite spot was "upriver," near Castella. Ben Jr. was the last Golinsky to live in Kennett.

Chapter 15

Memorable Personalities

A certain amount of rivalry between Charles Butters and the Golinsky family has been a theme over the years in the saga of Kennett. Butters and Golinsky were considered the foremost builders, movers, and shakers of the community. As previously noted, Charles Butters had resettled in Kennett after his successful stay in South Africa. It was widely believed that he had made a large fortune there. Certainly, he spent lavishly upon his return to Kennett. He had bought up much land, including about half of the lots in the town proper as well as over 6,000 acres of surrounding land.

These 6,000 acres were purchased prior to 1900, with the expectation that gold was abundant, but with no realization that copper was beneath his feet (Jones, 1985). He had reestablished his reduction works in Kennett. These were very busy and made him a great deal of money. The sale of land and water rights for the new Mammoth Smelter also brought in a small fortune.

The Kennett Water Company was a monopoly owned by Charles Butters. By 1914, he controlled all local sources of water except for the Golinsky Springs at Bernhard and a few other local springs located on individual pieces of property. In 1889 Charles Butters had begun to build "Butters' Ditch," as it was dubbed, a flume bringing water from Big Backbone Creek to his milling works. At that time he also had built a dam across the waterway that allowed him to regulate its flow. This was the source of the water sold by Kennett Water Company which was also called Kennett Water Works.

Charles Butters, since beginning his residence in Kennett, had long cherished the dream of creating a small, perfectly planned little city. His main obstacle was that Kennett was already established when he returned there from South Africa. The general plan of the neighborhoods and pattern of the streets had already been determined, albeit in a somewhat haphazard manner. In order to pursue his plan, he had to outflank the existing town.

His first move was to try to move the center of activity and settlement from Railroad Avenue and Lawson Street up to Butters Avenue. This was a new street running from the railroad east of Lawson Street, which was to be named Main Street. Mr. Butters had most of the street graded and paved, and a drainage system built along side. This carried rainwater as well as water from the small creek that ran down the hill parallel to the new street. The drainage would go under the railroad tracks and empty into the Sacramento River. Several brick business buildings were built at the lower end of this new Main Street, near Railroad Avenue. A corner, two-story brick structure was called the Butters Building; it became one of the longest standing buildings in Kennett.

As mentioned earlier, Charles Butters also established a new subdivision bearing his name within the township of Kennett. It was located up the hill and away from Railroad Avenue. This subdivision occurred at the same time that the Golinskys announced the newly planned town site named Bernhard, after its founder. Bernhard was located not far from the smelter and was intended as a nice but reasonably priced housing area for workers at the Mammoth Smelter.

Residences planned by Charles Butters in the new part of Kennett began at the northern end of Main Street. The hilly terrain here lent itself to terraced grounds on which it was expected that numerous villas would be built (*Free Press* "Annual," April 1905). Another scenic series of home sites was planned at

Mother Butters' Ranch located beyond the upper end of Butters Avenue. This area was part of the original 160 acres homestead owned by Mrs. S. L. Butters, mother of Charles.

Mr. Butters made it clear that he was building a high class, family-oriented community. He was creating an "uptown," advertised as far superior to the older parts of Kennett, or that is, the downtown. The ads that appeared in the local papers for Bernhard Golinsky's property and Charles Butters' property emphasized this difference.

The most important elements in Charles Butters' plans were the creation of a fine water system and the building of a large electric power plant to supply a steady amount of power to the homes and businesses in this new section of Kennett. The source of the water system was Big Backbone Creek. As noted earlier Mr. Butters already had erected an eighty-five foot dam across the creek, a project that had been carried out by Ira Merrill. A ditch gate in this dam was to divert water into a four and one-half mile, six-foot wide ditch along the right side of the creek. It was then to flow into a filtration reservoir built behind the Mammoth Smelter. From this reservoir a four-inch main that was over one-half mile long carried water across Big Backbone Creek to yet another reservoir for the town's water supply. A four-inch main carried this water down Butters Avenue to Railroad Avenue. It was thought to have enough pressure to be of use in fighting fires.

Butters had plans for an electrical power plant that would utilize a horseshoe bend in the Sacramento River. It was located a few miles above Kennett, but was situated well within Butters' huge property. In a distance of two and one-half miles this bend brought the river to a distance of 225 feet from where it had passed above. Around 1885, a tunnel had been started at this spot by miners hoping to use the water pressure from such a tunnel to clean bedrock for placer gold hydraulic mining. Butters proposed an electrical generation plant. Had it been completed, this plant would have brought Charles Butters in direct conflict with the

Northern California Power Company that brought electricity to Kennett by June 1905. This loop also was used by the Southern Pacific Railroad and it is still known as the Cantara Loop.

In a town overflowing with bars and saloons, the most popular establishment in Kennett, and famous up and down the West Coast, was the Diamond Bar. It was named for its owner, Victor E. "Slim" Warrens, known for his passion for diamonds. There is disagreement among old timers as to the exact details of Slim's past, or the exact date that he arrived in Kennett. However, most agree that Slim had an impoverished childhood and that in his youth he wandered about the West.

He seemed to have raised his stake for the Diamond Bar by bartending for others by day and gambling by night. He had just started his place in Kennett, located on the south side of Railroad Avenue a few houses from the depot, when it was destroyed by the great fire of December 3, 1904. In less than thirty minutes, all his work had been wiped out. But, by February 1905, Warrens had reestablished himself by rebuilding his new place on top of the old. A great deal of dirt was being excavated across Railroad Avenue for the building of the Trinity Copper Company offices. Slim bought this dirt and carted it across the street to fill up the street to a level with his building, greatly improving the appearance of Railroad Avenue.

Slim improved his new building using brick instead of wood and erecting a firewall between his property and the next one. The enlarged and improved bar opened on March 2, 1906. It served dinner to a crowd of 200 men (*Free Press,* March 2, 1906). The food service was overseen by Peter Ramsey. In February of 1907 Warrens added a forty-two room annex to his building. This went down the hill toward the river. He put double walls between the rooms and bought a huge asbestos awning to be dropped down the front of his building. It would stop all heat from a fire and could be rolled up when not needed.

No Service Less Than 10c. Secure a check from your waiter.

General Bill *of* Fare

STEAKS AND CHOPS

Plain Steak	25	Pork Chops	25
Rib Steak	35	Fried Liver	25
Sirloin	40	Liver and Bacon	25
T-Bone	50	Liver and Onions	25
Fried Ham	25	Hamburger	25
Fried Bacon	25	Pork Sausage	25
French Lamb Chop on Toast	30	Side Order of Bacon or Ham	15
Mutton Chops	25	Side Order of Mushrooms	25
Boiled Salt Mackerel	35	Boiled Salmon Belly	35

VEGETABLES

Green Peas	10	Fried Onions	10
String Beans	10	Lyonnaise	10
Sugar Corn	10	Saratoga Chips	10
Stewed Tomatoes	10	German Fried	10
Minced Potatoes	10	Shoe Strings	10
French Fried Potatoes	10		

EGGS AND OMELETTES

Boiled .....(3) (2)	25	Omelette with Cheese or Fresh Tomatoes	40
Fried .....(3) (2)	25	Ham Omelette	35
Scrambled, Plain	25	Spanish Omelette	35
With Tomatoes or Cheese	40	Jelly Omelette	40
Shirred, Plain	30	Rum Omelette	40
Poached Eggs and Toast	30	Oyster Omelette	45
Ham and Eggs	25	With Mushrooms	50
Bacon and Eggs	25		
Plain Omelette	30		

CEREALS AND BREAKFAST DISHES

French Toast	25	Shredded Wheat	15
Dry Toast	10	Cakes and Pies, per cut	05
Milk Toast	15	Hot Cakes, Syrup and Coffee	15
Grape Nuts	15	German Pancake	40
Force	15		

SANDWICHES

Roast Lamb or Beef	10	Hot Cheese on Toast	15
Egg	10	Sardine	15
Fried or Boiled Ham	10	Hamburger	10
Ham and Egg	15	Limburger	15
Tongue	10	American Cheese	15
Cheese	10		

Bread, Butter, Vegetables, Cup Coffee, Tea or Glass of Milk included with above orders.

Please report any incivility or inat-tention

Food list from the Diamond Bar. (Courtesy of Golinsky family)

The interior of the bar was an artistic triumph. The actual bar, made of mahogany with a marble base, was fifty feet long and had a rail of walnut six inches thick. Clean towels hung along the length of the rail for hand wiping and were changed frequently. The ceiling was covered with carvings and inlay work. Numerous diamonds (or glass beads) sparkled from the walls and ceiling.

The paintings of nude women that also adorned the walls were another popular attraction. These were done by an itinerant painter who was said to have been trained in Paris. His subject matter lent credence to this rumor. Lighting came from bunches of glass grapes (which still exist) that were also imported from

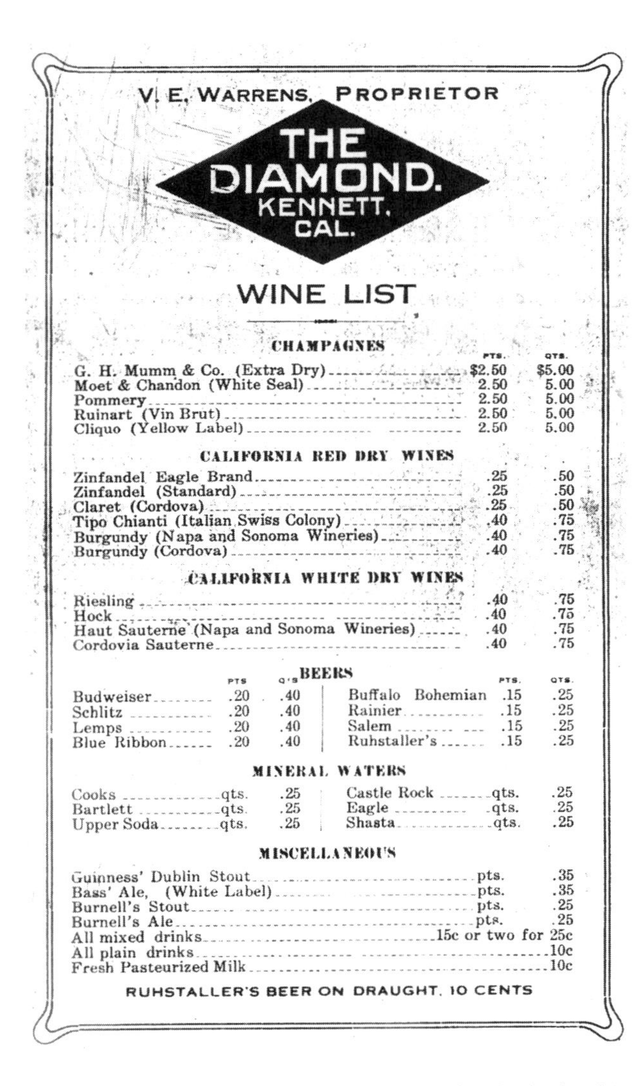

V. E. WARRENS, PROPRIETOR

THE DIAMOND. KENNETT, CAL.

WINE LIST

CHAMPAGNES

	PTS.	QTS.
G. H. Mumm & Co. (Extra Dry)	$2.50	$5.00
Moet & Chandon (White Seal)	2.50	5.00
Pommery	2.50	5.00
Ruinart (Vin Brut)	2.50	5.00
Cliquo (Yellow Label)	2.50	5.00

CALIFORNIA RED DRY WINES

Zinfandel Eagle Brand	.25	.50
Zinfandel (Standard)	.25	.50
Claret (Cordova)	.25	.50
Tipo Chianti (Italian Swiss Colony)	.40	.75
Burgundy (Napa and Sonoma Wineries)	.40	.75
Burgundy (Cordova)	.40	.75

CALIFORNIA WHITE DRY WINES

Riesling	.40	.75
Hock	.40	.75
Haut Sauterne (Napa and Sonoma Wineries)	.40	.75
Cordovia Sauterne	.40	.75

BEERS

	PTS	Q'S		PTS.	QTS.
Budweiser	.20	.40	Buffalo Bohemian	.15	.25
Schlitz	.20	.40	Rainier	.15	.25
Lemps	.20	.40	Salem	.15	.25
Blue Ribbon	.20	.40	Ruhstaller's	.15	.25

MINERAL WATERS

Cooks	qts.	.25	Castle Rock	qts.	.25
Bartlett	qts.	.25	Eagle	qts.	.25
Upper Soda	qts.	.25	Shasta	qts.	.25

MISCELLANEOUS

Guinness' Dublin Stout	pts.	.35
Bass' Ale, (White Label)	pts.	.35
Burnell's Stout	pts.	.25
Burnell's Ale	pts.	.25
All mixed drinks		15c or two for 25c
All plain drinks		10c
Fresh Pasteurized Milk		10c

RUHSTALLER'S BEER ON DRAUGHT, 10 CENTS

Wine list from the Diamond Bar. (Courtesy of Golinsky family)

France. Beer was drawn from a large keg into mugs. Whiskey was drawn from a one hundred and fifty gallon keg into demijohns encased in heavy leather. As business increased, Slim added an upper floor to his building and served food that gained a reputation for being both extremely tasty and remarkably inexpensive.

Slim Warrens became one of Kennett's best known and respected citizens. Although he was a man of rather simple personal tastes in most matters, he sported a large number of diamonds on his clothing. He would consider diamonds as legal tender at his poker table. It was customary for him to wear an enormous stickpin and a very large ring. These diamonds, as one would expect, attracted a number of robbers who, however, lived to regret any encounter with Slim. Once, when he was threatened by a gun, Slim threw his diamonds down the bar drain and then chased the would-be robber from his premises (McKim, 1985).

On November 21, 1912, Frank Brownlee was arrested in Hilt and confessed that he was the leader in the hold ups of Victor Warrens and the robbery of his safe. Warrens' $1,500 diamond pin was located at a lodging house in Ashland, Oregon. At that time also found was Warren's watch and Brownlee's gun, which was thought to have been used in a murder in August 1912. In April 1913 a second holdup man, Charles Lewis (aka Earl Newton) was arrested in Chico, California. He soon joined his partner in Folsom Prison.

Despite this oddity in his dress, Slim Warrens developed a reputation for fairness. He himself would not gamble with his customers and was said to have discouraged people who could not afford it from doing so. He made his fortune from the proceeds of his dining room, bar, and gambling tables. He wisely invested his earnings in real estate outside Kennett in case the rumors he had heard about a large dam turned out to be true, and he indulged himself in his fondness for diamonds.

Only one story surfaced about a time when Slim was drawn into a poker game (McKim, 1985). A meeting was arranged between Slim and a famous outlaw, the Denver Kid. At this game, the Kid seemed to have won all the money from the other players as well as Slim's diamonds. In discussing this matter, Slim and the other local players felt that they had been somehow cheated. A few days later, Slim appeared in his bar wearing all his diamonds and the other players gradually admitted that they had recovered their money. No one ever obtained an exact explanation for this turn of events.

Chapter 16

World War I, the Depression, and Prohibition

During 1912, ominous news from Europe had indicated that a great war was in the offing. Such rumors encouraged full production at the mines and smelters. This also encouraged Ben and Rosa to seek the greater comfort of their apartment in San Francisco. They rented their house in Kennett to Mr. and Mrs. Frank Meixner. In July of 1913 Bernhard suffered a sudden heart attack while visiting a drug store in San Francisco. He recovered from this attack and seemed to be doing well.

On February 15, 1914, Bernhard's seventy-first birthday, Ben and Rosa posed for a portrait on their way to a celebratory lunch at the Cliff House. In this picture, they certainly looked hale and hearty. However, just one week later, on February 28, 1914, Bernhard literally dropped dead in his San Francisco home. Bernhard's obituary in the *Courier Free Press* was long, detailed, and laudatory. It praised his fairness, generosity, and his devotion to his family and to Kennett. The Father of Kennett was dead!

In his will Bernhard left everything to Rosa. She was grief-stricken over the loss of her lifelong companion. When she pulled herself together, she returned to Kennett where the many Golinsky interests needed her attention. She leased the Kennet Hotel because it was too big a burden for her. She settled into her Kennett house, adopted two fierce looking dogs, and evaluated her mining interests. The Golinsky Mining Company was becoming very active as copper for armaments and war material was in great demand.

Rosa and Bernhard Golinsky, February 1914. (Courtesy of Golinsky family)

In June 1914, Mount Lassen erupted. Plumes of smoke were visible over Shasta and Tehama counties. The eruption called national attention to Mount Lassen. Later in the year, it was designated a national park, lying in four counties: Shasta, Lassen, Plumas, and Tehama.

In August 1914, Germany declared war on Russia and World War I began. During the first months of the war, there was little change in the lives of the people of northern California. In fact, familiar interests and local events dominated daily life.

Although the Coram Smelter had closed down in 1911, the Farmers' Protective Association continued its complaints about fumes and continued to attack the Mammoth Smelter. In 1913, several bills concerning control of smelter fumes had come before the state legislature. Only one bill passed (Kristophers, 1973). In this bill, control of smelters was given to the state Board of Health. The farmers sought to get funds to fight a legal battle against the Mammoth Smelter. The director of the United States

The widowed Rosa Golinsky and her canine companions. (Courtesy Golinsky family)

Bureau of Mines, Dr. J. A. Holmes, visited the Mammoth Smelter and admitted that the bag houses were not controlling fumes. They were as big a failure as the gigantic chimneys (circa 1905) had been.

Although the farmers lacked funds, they continued with plans to take the Mammoth Company to court. Despite the war in Europe, in November 1914 the farmers started proceedings against the company. Their case was heard by Judge William Van Fleet, a judge known to be sympathetic toward the copper companies. In March of 1915, to no one's surprise, the judge decided in favor of the Mammoth Company. This defeat ended five years of efforts by the Shasta County Farmers' Protective Association, which was now discouraged and in debt. The Mammoth Company continued to operate its mines, but much of the ore was now being shipped elsewhere for smelting, a large part going to the ASARCO smelter near Tacoma, Washington.

The war raging in Europe caused a sharp rise in copper prices. This created a new mining boom in Shasta County. Kristophers related that "more copper was mined in Shasta County during the war years than any other comparable period of time" (1973, p. 80). The Golinsky Mining Company had its most active years during the war, as copper was needed for armaments and war material. Many new workers were hired by all of the mines in the area. The United States entered the war in April 1917 after the sinking of the *Lusitania* by German U boats. No Kennett men were killed in the war; locally the effect of the war was prosperity and full employment.

In October 1914, Kennett was struck by another large fire near the railroad station. It was said to have been started by an oil lamp in a building near McGuire's drug store. The Kennett band was playing when the fire broke out. They stopped in the middle of a piece, and helped the firemen up onto the vantage point of the bandstand, where they sent streams of water onto the Kennet Hotel, saving it. The fire swept up the Lawson Street hill destroying everything else in its path. The fire spread rapidly due to strong winds from the south and the lack of sufficient water to fight the fire. The town held a meeting two days later in which it was decided to rebuild Kennett as soon as the insurance was adjusted. Everyone decided to rebuild, except David Endicott. This was the third time he had been burned out in Kennett. He was tired of rebuilding and decided to retire to some farm property outside of the town.

The volunteer fire department complained to the city trustees that there had not been enough water to fight the fire. It stopped burning, they said, due to the lack of more material to burn, not from being doused with sufficient water. The Kennett Water Company (Mr. Butters' monopoly) had failed to deliver.

World War I ended with the November 11, 1918, armistice. The relief and joy that the terrible war was over was soon tempered by the economic downturn well underway by 1919. The many factories, coal and copper mines, and expanded railroad lines were too large for a peacetime economy and a great depression developed. The Mammoth Company closed its smelter in May 1919. The mine itself was kept open for several years thereafter. Ore was taken by rail to the ASARCO smelter in Tacoma, Washington. The Mammoth Smelter reopened briefly in 1923, but was closed forever shortly thereafter. Hundreds of people suddenly found themselves without work, and left Kennett to search for employment elsewhere. Houses were abandoned leaving outstanding mortgages and unpaid taxes.

In 1919, with the closing of the smelter, the Mammoth Company also closed its hospital, which had served not only Mammoth company employees but also the rest of Kennett. A group of physicians remaining in Kennett leased a section of the old Kennett (Golinsky) Hotel and made it into a hospital. Previous to this the hotel had been leased out by Rosa Golinsky to various Kennett people, including that enterprising businesswoman, Madelina Carattini. It had proved too large and needed too much upkeep to make money. Later, it briefly served as the hospital.

As the depression deepened more people left Kennett. In the early 1920s the hotel furnishings had been sold off and in 1926, the shell of the hotel was bought by Jake Penturff of Redding, a former early Kennett resident. He dismantled it piece by piece. By horse and wagon, he took the lumber to Redding, where he built four cottages. As they became abandoned, Kennett's other houses and buildings began to disappear. Many houses accidentally caught fire and were left to burn to the ground. Several houses were torn down and the lumber shipped elsewhere. Kennett settled into a period of gloom and steady decline. The atmosphere was ominous.

After the end of WWI, many hardships were felt. There was widespread unemployment and to cap all of these hardships one of life's simple pleasures became illegal. In 1919 the Congress of the United States passed the Volstead Act, which became the Eighteenth Amendment to the Constitution. The act became law at 12:01 A.M., January 17, 1920. It forbade the manufacture, sale, import, or export of intoxicating liquors. It is probably safe to say that from the very moment this Prohibition law passed, a flourishing underground trade in liquor was established throughout the country. For its part, the government hired armed men to search for and destroy illegal stills. These men were called "Prohi's" and became a thoroughly hated group.

Of course, many residents of Kennett and environs got into the business of making and selling bootleg liquor. They went to extreme lengths to conceal their operations from the Prohi's, who hid in the hills and swooped down on their suspects. The Prohi's were very zealous in enforcing law. At one time, they raided a Jewish synagogue in Redding, and confiscated sacramental wine. Another time a wagonload of barrels of wine being hauled to Kennett and said to be for sacramental purposes was halted at Red Bluff by the sheriff. He poured the wine into a sewer. In June 1923, the Prohi's swooped down on Kennett and arrested a group of business people for violating the Volsted Act. Among those charged were two Balma brothers and Mrs. Madelina Carattini!

Victor Warrens of the famous Diamond Bar decided to store his first class brews in a San Francisco bonded warehouse. Maybe he would sell it at some later date to the medicinal drug trade. Meanwhile his famous bar was changed into a restaurant, and became well-known for the railroad sandwich. This consisted of bologna and cheese between hunks of French bread. It sold for thirty-five cents and included a mug of near beer.

Kennett now had too few residents to qualify any longer as an incorporated city, so in 1931 Kennett disincorporated. In 1933, the Twenty-first Amendment to the United States Constitution was passed, repealing Prohibition. This event caused general jubilation, but was too late to do much for Kennett. The Kennett Bank, a branch of the First Savings Bank of Shasta County in Redding had been closed since the fall of 1925. The vault had been taken under guard to Redding.

One of the few enterprises to show some life during this great depression was the Golinsky Mine. It had been idle through the 1920s, and at some date between 1924 and 1931 Rosa sold off the controlling shares of the Golinsky Copper Company stock to W. D. Tillotson. He became president of the company. He also

Broken leaching tanks at the Golinsky Mine from its last phase of mining operated by the Vickery brothers, 1931–35. (Courtesy of Frank Viscaino)

become the owner of seven of the original claims that he himself had patented with the federal Patent Office in Washington, D.C. (Mining Patents, vol. 14, p. 374, Shasta County Recorder). In 1931 he leased the Golinsky Mine to brothers H. M. and W. C. Vickery, who intended to mine the overlying sulfide ore for gold. They signed a twenty-five-year contract giving a ten percent royalty to the Golinsky Copper Company (Official Records, vol. 76, p. 253, Shasta County Recorder).

The Vickery brothers invested heavily in the United States Gausen Mine, popularly known as the Golinsky Mine, constructing a treatment plant using plate amalgamation, which proved a failure. Next they built structures to use a cyanide leaching process. Others, including the Iron Mountain Mine, had been successful with this method. Several storms in the winter of 1931–32 destroyed many of their improvements before the plant could be completed. The Vickery brothers sold their lease to the Backbone Mining Company in the fall of 1932 for $10 (Official Records, vol. 76, Shasta County Recorder). In return the Backbone Mining Company assumed the $15,000 debt built up by the Vickerys. This sale was approved by the Golinsky Copper Company, which drew up a new lease with the Backbone Mining Company and gave them an option to buy the property within four years for $15,000. This agreement was signed in January 1935 (Official Records, vol. 76, Shasta County Recorder)

The Backbone Mining Company also invested considerable money in the Golinsky Mine. A road replacing the trail was built from the mine to the limestone quarry in 1935 (Kinkel et al., 1956). A small smelter was built; other buildings were fixed up and mining began in 1936–37. Two existing adits were located and explored. The ore was smelted to form a concentrated material that was shipped to the American Smelting and Refining Company's smelter in Tacoma. According to the Backbone Mining Company, the matter leaving the smelter had thirteen grams copper, two ounces gold, and twenty ounces silver per ton (Elliott, 1981).

These encouraging results were not enough to take care of expenses and earn some profit, so the mine was idle again in 1938. A mine employee filed a lien to collect wages against the Golinsky Copper Company (Book of Liens, no. 5, p. 432, Shasta County Recorder). No further work was done at the Golinsky Mine after 1938, except for dismantling the smelter and reduction works between 1938–1944 (Kinkel et al., 1956). The Backbone Mining Company's effort was the last mining activity at the Golinsky Mine. That this was indeed the last effort was assured by the building of Shasta Dam, and the resultant flooding of Kennett.

Chapter 17

Shasta Dam and the End of Kennett

The idea of a dam to solve California's water problems had been forming in many minds for several generations as the path leading to an agricultural empire in California. Talk of damming the Sacramento River above the confluence with the Pit for irrigation and flood control had been considered since the end of the Civil War. During President Grant's administration, engineers were sent to investigate sites and, as mentioned earlier, in 1887 the *Free Press* reported an investigative boat trip down the Sacramento in which the explorers spent the night with Jake Golinsky at Kennett.

As previously noted, for years many people had recognized the need to control the temperamental waters of the Sacramento River and the abundant rainfall in the area. A place to receive the excess water eventually became the northern branch of the Central Valley Project. Dozens of agencies, both private and governmental, studied, surveyed, and investigated the Central Valley. The problem was obvious—there was too much water in the North, and not enough in the South. As said at the time, "they needed to move the rain," (Allen, 1987, p. 13) a sentiment frequently mentioned in earlier times by Rosa Golinsky.

Around 1873 the engineers sent by President Grant made a report to Congress, but decades went by; more studies were made.

This activity barely ruffled the feathers of Kennett residents. Meanwhile the idea grew outside of Kennett that a huge dam, not a series of small ones, was needed to adequately solve the water problem. Selection of a dam site required more years of engineering studies and economic analyses. Few engineers felt bold enough to propose what became the present site, because of its difficulties, size, and resultant costs.

Sites considered were: (1) The Baird site on the Pit River five miles upstream from Kennett; (2) The Table Mountain site on the Sacramento River, ten miles up from Red Bluff; and (3) The Kennett site, three miles downstream from Kennett, where a durable rock existed in two ridges forming a very obtuse V with the point upstream (McKim, p. 122).

The Kennett site was soon considered the ideal one because of the constriction caused by the solid rock on either side of the ninety-degree turn of the Sacramento River at this spot. In addition, the area behind the proposed dam, with its multiple rivers contributing water, would supply enough water to create a reservoir and still not deprive the river of an adequate flow. What would also happen was a situation only mentioned obliquely by the United States government: Kennett and the seven other local mining communities would be flooded—washed away—washed off the map! The highway and the railroad tracks and bridge across the Pit river would also become flooded and have to be moved. The small Kennett cemetery would also have to be moved. Wintu Indian sites would be buried forever. There is no record of any public hearings held on the choice of the site. Perhaps the diminished population of Kennett; the loss by attrition of many homes and buildings was one of the factors in deciding on this site.

The government set about acquiring the property needed for the dam as well as that area which would be flooded by its waters. In the August 1935 Rivers and Harbors Bill, $12 million was

The abandoned Mammoth Smelter c. 1936. Ballast for the relocated highway and railroad beds was taken from the rubble left by the 1919 destruction of the smelter. (Courtesy of the United States Department of Interior)

authorized to begin construction of what was then called the Kennett Dam, later changed to Shasta Dam.

The federal government continued to fund the project for many years. In 1935 $20 million was appropriated by the Bureau of Reclamation to start construction. The eventual total of appropriations reached $173 million by the opening of Shasta Dam, June 17, 1950.

The Bureau of Reclamation began work on the projected dam in November 1935. Construction of camp facilities began in 1937. Work on the dam itself began in September 1938, and the relocation of the Southern Pacific railroad tracks around the anticipated outlines of the reservoir began in October 1938. Ballast for the relocated roadbed was taken from the piles of rubble left by the 1919 destruction of the Mammoth Smelter.

The highway also had to be relocated. To achieve this move of railroad and highway, the highest double-decked bridge in the world, the Pit River Bridge, was built to get both trains and motor vehicles across the Pit River arm of the reservoir, to be called Shasta Lake. This bridge currently carries Amtrak trains, freight trains, and vehicles using Interstate 5.

It is almost impossible to visualize the vast dam building project. Whole new villages were constructed with schools and stores to accommodate the thousands of workers and their families. These towns were to be called Shasta Dam Village and Boomtown, among other names. In 1936 the U.S. Bureau of Reclamation hired B. D. Glaha, photographer, to photograph the entire dam site, and any natural and man-made features that might have an impact on either supplying or building the dam. Glaha spent weeks taking pictures. His greatest shock was seeing the smelters and mining sites and the miles of denuded hillsides.

There was little difficulty in acquiring title to the actual dam site. But, behind the proposed dam were towns, resorts, highways, and railroads that would be flooded. Many people sold their property to the government willingly; others were reluctant to leave their homes, and they waited for water to lap over roads on their property, and then they fled in haste. Some people took advantage of the situation, and early on sold the valuables that could be moved. Many people believed even at this date, 1936, that the dam never would be built. Others tried to make any money from the situation they could.

After Congress had passed the Rivers and Harbors Act in 1935, the planning and construction of the dam and dam site proceeded nonstop. The United States Bureau of Reclamation oversaw the tremendous project. The railroad tracks would interfere with construction, and later would be covered with water from the forming of Shasta Lake. The relocation of the railroad about five miles east also necessitated building new tunnels to replace those to be flooded. The cemetery was relocated to a small plot near Project City.

By 1943 most of the road from Kennett to the Golinsky Mine was under water. For a short time as the reservoir (Shasta Lake) was filling, the Bureau of Reclamation ran a barge-ferry service across the lake to carry trucks of ore and other traffic and act as a replacement for the road. This arrangement was awkward and unsatisfactory; the ferry was not available twenty-four hours a day, caused delays, and was costly.

Since 1940 W. D. Tillotson, as president of the Golinsky Copper Company and legal representative of the stockholders, had been carrying on a lively correspondence with the Bureau of Reclamation. Rosa Golinsky had died in 1930 and Mr. Tillotson was now the owner of the largest share of the company's stock. My mother Rubie (Radzinski) Blumenthal held the next largest share, followed by Ray Golinsky, widow of Charles; Flora Gilman, widow of Jake; the heirs of Hennie Gans; and then my mother's sister, Ethel. Perhaps the fact that my mother held the largest share of any family member can be traced back to Fritz Weischmann's verbal bequest to my mother, as he lay dying from the train accident. The stock might have represented Uncle Bernard keeping his promise.

W. D. Tillotson, on behalf of the Golinsky heirs, offered to sell the road right-of-way to the government for $17,000, because the flooded road made the mine almost worthless. This proposal was reviewed and rereviewed with no action taken.

On March, 28, 1944, writing to Charles E. Carey, regional director of the U.S. Bureau of Reclamation, Tillotson said:

> ... I am compelled to call the matter to your attention myself as president and chief owner of the Golinsky Copper Company.
>
> I am now eighty-three years old and I am nearing the end of

> the trail. I have been contributing substantially to this republic for more than sixty years and now the government destroys some of my property and I feel that it should promptly recompense me for the damage done. I am not asking this for myself. There are five old ladies that own three-fifths of the stock of the Golinsky Copper Company. They inherited their interest from the late Benard [*sic*] and Rosa Golinsky who were pioneers of the town of Kennett. I am the only one who knows the details and history of the Golinsky Mine and I want the matter settled soon to relive my mind so I will not have to think about it anymore.

By July 1944 Mr. Tillotson was getting more impatient and … old. As he wrote, "I have informed you that my associates are all old ladies and I am now in my 84 year. … I will recommend to my associates … that it will be for our best interests to convey the whole property to the government if we receive a sum of $20,000" (correspondence with Bureau of Reclamation, 1944). The government knew a good deal when it saw one and so the whole Golinsky Mine property was conveyed to the government for only $3,000 more than just the road right-of-way. On September 20, 1944, the Golinsky Group of patented mining claims on 164.75 acres of land, and a road easement to Kennett, became the property of the United States government, sold by the Golinsky Copper Company (OR vol. 222, p. 109 Shasta County Recorder). As mentioned earlier, the last work on the mine after 1938 had been the dismantling of the Vickery brothers' smelter sometime between 1938 and 1944 (Kinkel et al., 1956).

Most Golinsky properties (houses, lots, etc.) within Kennett proper had been sold many years ago to the state of California in lieu of delinquent taxes. Some of Rosa's debts went back to 1898! Mrs. Charles Golinsky (Ray) had property that had been sold to the state in 1926 for delinquent taxes from 1921. Ben Jr. was still a resident of Kennett when he died in 1921.

Rosa continued to live in San Francisco. In her last years she continued to make her oil-painted candles, which she distributed to her relatives, who responded with gratitude regardless of their true feelings. She died there at the age of eighty-six on March 25, 1930. The descendents of the Golinskys of Kennett are scattered, but a large group live in the San Francisco Bay Area. Ben Jr., the last Golinsky in Kennett, died July 9, 1921, in a Redding hospital. The direct heirs of Jake Golinsky, including grandchildren, now all bear the last name of Gilman, a name change achieved officially by Jake in 1918 when he relocated in San Francisco.

The only remaining physical evidence of the Golinskys in Kennett is the Golinsky Mine, the sale of which had been negotiated by Mr. Tillotson in 1944. Since then it has been administered by the United States Forest Service. When the reservoir filled in 1944, all access to the mine was cut off, except via boat across Shasta Lake and then making a long, steep and dangerous hike. Some sporadic efforts by individuals to enter the old adits and look for gold have been reported. Needless to say the old diggings are partly fallen in and very dangerous. As for gold—ask the Golinskys, the Vickerys, the Backbone mining people. The idea of a fortune in gold is a universal but often illusory dream.

For residents of Kennett by 1938, it had become obvious that their homes would be buried under hundreds of feet of water. An ironic sidelight to this is the activity of Charles Butters' Kennett Water Company. Throughout the late '20s and early '30s, the water company kept dunning its customers to pay delinquent water bills. People understood very well that there was going to be more water than they could handle within a few years, and saw no reason to pay for any now.

Charles Butters, residing in San Francisco, kept up a lively correspondence with W. W. Middleton, his representative in Kennett. There was much discussion between Middleton and Butters, who wanted to tap into the Golinsky Springs to supple-

The last residents of Lawson Street reluctant to leave Kennett, c. 1942. (Courtesy of United States Department of Interior)

ment his Ditch. Using an all-gravity system, the springs could supply the current (much reduced) needs of the town.

The rights of the ownership of the Golinsky Springs dates back to January 1916 when Rosa Golinsky had sold to Antone Carattini, son of Madelina:

> All those certain water and water-rights situate in the town site of Bernhard and Kennett … known as and called the "Golinsky Springs," consisting of three separate and distinct springs of water together with all of the waters … and sufficient ground … to enable said party of the second part to collect and divert the waters … into pipes. … (Book 124, Deeds, Shasta County, p. 169).

There is a gap in available records at this point, leaving questions as to what had happened to the Butters Ditch, and in what manner Mr. Butters had obtained rights to use the Golinsky Springs, which seemed to have been sold to the Carattinis in 1916.

In 1928 Butters had offered Vic Warrens of the Diamond Bar a chance to buy the Kennett Water Company. Warrens felt that Butters' offer was shabby, that he was devaluing the importance of the water supply. Butters for his part commented on the exaggerated value that Warrens put on businesses in Kennett. Both seem to have been playing a game; by 1928 there was enough evidence floating around about the building of a huge dam and its consequences for Kennett. In August 1931 in a report to Mr. Butters, Mr. Middleton mentioned the Vickery brothers' lease on the Golinsky Mine. He said that Kennett had only received thirty-four inches of rain for the season, half of normal! The Golinsky Springs were holding up, supplying more water than the pipe

Butters' brick building housing the post office and built to survive for the ages, waits for the Shasta Dam water to reach it. (Courtesy United States Department of Interior)

could carry. Mr. Middleton also mentioned that the Golinsky Springs were not interfering with springs being discovered by Madelina Carattini, nor she with them. Despite the now understood fate of Kennett and the other towns in the area, Madelina Carattini had been buying up houses and lots in large numbers. She must have had some plan to profit from the flooding of Kennett. Perhaps she felt she could buy the properties for a trifle and then be reimbursed by the government at a higher price.

The true value of Kennett's condemned property was settled in 1940 when the Bureau of Reclamation, Department of Interior, issued an appraisal report on all property in and adjoining the town site of Kennett. Any property reimbursements by the government for loss of property due to flooding caused by Shasta Dam would be based on this appraisal. In this report Madelina Carattini is listed as owning five lots in the town of Kennett, all but one lot in the town of Bernhard and ten lots in the West Kennett addition to Bernhard. Whether she was reimbursed for all of this land is yet to be known. She also spent time, energy, and money suing Rosa Golinsky, and, since Rosa's death in 1930, her estate, for reimbursement for Golinsky property that she felt was hers. Her claims held up the final probate of Rosa's will until 1942, and by that time Madelina too was dead and her executrix was suing Rosa's executor (her nephew Richard Gilman). Unfortunately, I do not have the records that would unravel this whole story.

In 1938, when the U.S. government ordered the removal or destruction of all buildings left in Kennett, there was a flurry of activity among the few remaining property owners. The decorations of Slim Warrens' Diamond Bar had been famous in the days of Kennett's prosperity. Now, faced with imminent destruction, their removal became a minor crisis. Several people wanted to buy the famous mahogany bar, but it was too large for normal transportation. By the time World War II began, there were no large trucks available to haul it. In 1943 water backed up by the dam began slapping at the base of Warrens' building. The building was sold for scrap to James McKenna of Redding and E. E. Isley of Anderson. Some of the fixtures went to Ralph Grace, who removed the famous murals. Isley disputed Grace's ownership, so Grace gave the murals back to Isley, who is said to have stored them in a barn. In 1962 he sold them to Charles Gleeson, who stored them in a warehouse, where they were destroyed by fire in 1964. The glass grapes enjoy existence today in the Sunset Bar in Toyon, on the road to Shasta Dam. The Sunset's mahogany bar is a somewhat smaller copy of the original bar. The original object had been sold to Mrs. Madelina Carattini, who never had a chance to try to move it to an establishment that she owned near Kennett, before the Diamond Bar caught fire. Arguments are still being heard by old timers about the origin of this mysterious fire. The building itself is now under Lake Shasta.

Other memories of its former glory persist. In 1999 two Redding businessmen opened a brewery, ale house and restaurant, called the Diamond Bar. Located in the older more picturesque business section of Redding, it is decorated with photos of old Kennett. Its atmosphere reflects the friendliness and informality of its namesake.

Mr. Tillotson, for his part, resumed his law practice in Redding. There he was a well-known and, even at a distance, an easily recognized local celebrity. He was extremely thin, very tall, and walked with a jerk. His law practice remained busy, in large part due to his reputation for integrity. It is told around Redding that in his ninetieth year, feeling too weak to appear in court, Mr. Tillotson tried a case over the telephone connected to Judge Richard Eaton's chambers. He won the case! He died in 1952 at the age of ninety-two.

Shasta Dam (formerly called Kennett Dam) under construction, 1941. (Courtesy Balma family)

The Kennet School also waits for to meet its fate. (Courtesy United States Department of Interior)

The rising water reaches Gold Nugget Cafe. (Courtesy United States Department of Interior)

The old Pit River Bridge drowning. The new (present) bridge that carries both trains and automobiles is towering in the background, 1944. (Courtesy of United States Department of Interior)

Shasta Dam nearing completion as the lake fills, 1944. (Courtesy United States Department of Interior)

Contemporary view of dam, lake and Mount Shasta. Slaughter Island is the only remaining visible part of Kennett. Its name refers to the livestock kept there until needed for sale as meat by Kennett butchers. (Courtesy of Redding Convention and Visitors Bureau)

Chapter 18

Personal Recollections and Legacies of the Mines

While writing this history of Kennett, a memory gradually emerged. I *had* been through Kennett and on the railroad. In the summer of 1929 my mother, father, and I took a lengthy train trip from Chicago, traversing the Canadian Rockies, visiting Vancouver, B.C., and Victoria, and reentering the United States through Seattle. All this travel was done by train, bus, or ferry boat.

In Portland, Oregon, we boarded the famous Shasta Limited for the trip to California. By this time, it must have become obvious to the adults, or at least to my mother, that the train would go through Kennett. When I learned this I was thrilled, remembering my mother's wonderful tales. I thought the scenery would be beautiful, but my mother quickly told me that the smelter fumes had killed all the vegetation.

My father had bought one of the earliest movie cameras, so he set himself up in the observation car, where he regaled men sitting around sipping liquor from coffee cups (it was during Prohibition). By the time we approached Kennett, the observation car was crowded with happy sightseers, waiting to get a view of my mother's "childhood home." She had not seen it since she had left in 1907. My father stood on the small outside portion of the car; my mother, inside, stood near the center, nervous. I was also inside the car, not knowing which way to look. What took place next lasted less than five minutes. I recall it in a blur. The train entered a tunnel. I know now that it was Tunnel Number Two, just above Kennett.

When the train emerged it made its ninety-degree turn towards the west. A few unpainted shacks appeared, then the station and the brick post office. I remember a crossing sign resting at an uneasy forty-five degree angle. We crossed a small river (Backbone Creek), and the train began its second ninety-degree turn. As it was doing this, the ruins of the Mammoth Smelter became visible. And then we entered another tunnel (Number One). When the train came out of this tunnel, there was a second of stunned silence, and then a roar of raucous laughter. My mother fled in tears to our compartment. My father followed her and begged her forgiveness.

My mother's reactions were deep and conflicting. She was full of fond memories of her wonderful sojourn in Kennett. She was shocked by the sad condition of the remains of the town. Possibly being on the train that had formed the main artery of Kennett brought back memories of who had come and gone and those who had died on the tracks. The sightseers saw nothing of value worth saving in Kennett. This attitude resonated with the dam builders and land clearers. This devaluation of the town is in great contrast to the story of a later resident of the town, Diana Caneva Grenfell, published in *The Covered Wagon* (1989).

Grenfell was eleven years old when she spent the summer of 1938 with her uncle in Kennett. Her uncle had a small house he had built himself, with running water but an outhouse. He had goats, pigs, and a wonderful vegetable garden. He grew everything the family needed. There she spent the happiest days of her life, running free, swimming, fishing, climbing trees in abandoned orchards, picking the fruit and blackberries.

The town seemed a bit quiet to her, and the main event of her day was the walk to the post office. She has no recollection of any talk of the building of the dam. At the end of her stay she was hoping her uncle would invite her back for the next summer. She was shocked when he told her that these were his last weeks in Kennett. He had to move his belongings and find another place to live, as the dam building had started and the water was rising. He was one of the last residents to leave the town (*Covered Wagon*, 1989, pp. 78–81).

Perhaps the last resident of Kennett was Lawrence Bannon, who refused the order of the Bureau of Reclamation for everyone to leave. He spent several years on a houseboat floating on the rapidly growing lake, commuting in an outboard motorboat. When or if he left has not been established.

As Copper City, Delamar, Winthrop, Baird, Elmore, Morely, Heroult, Kennett, and numerous Wintu sites slowly disintegrated beneath the waters of Shasta Lake, memories of them faded and the lake and recreation area became a new scenic spot—a new reality.

But the abandoned mines above the lake on the hills west of it have a message of their own for all humankind. The message reads: WORLD'S "WORST WATER" FOUND NEAR REDDING—a headline from the *San Francisco Chronicle,* March 23, 2000. Already considered to be among the worst pollution sites in the United States, the vast underground tunnels of the Iron Mountain Mine is a federal Superfund cleanup site. The U.S. Geological Survey has been sampling runoff from this mine since about 1970. It became an Environmental Protection Agency Superfund site in 1990 when scientists discovered that Iron Mountain Mine at the site of Keswick had water so contaminated with sulfur that their instruments could not measure the acidity (or pH). A new instrument had to be devised and it showed the pH tested at a negative 3.6, making it the current record holder for an acid found outside a laboratory in a natural setting. Since water seeping from this mine leaks into the Sacramento River and becomes a part of Redding's drinking water, drastic measures were needed. Today the water is now scrubbed, filtered and treated with lime to reduce the acidity, and it is thus transformed into drinkable water. Horrible fish kills with thousands of dead fish flowing to shore used to be routine occurrences downhill from Iron Mountain. No large die-offs have occurred since the Superfund cleanup got under way.

As might be expected, other mines in this area also have running water flowing downhill year round, reaching Shasta Lake. This water is known as acid mine drainage (AMD), and flows come from the Mammoth Mine, the Golinsky Mine, and others. The largest amount of AMD comes from the Mammoth Mine smelter site. The Mammoth is on private land. Its cleanup has been ordered by the Environmental Protection Agency. The Golinsky property, through the settlement with the heirs negotiated by Mr. Tillotson in September 1944, is now owned by the U.S. Forest Service, which, as owner, also was ordered to clean up the AMD. Both mines have become Superfund sites. Accordingly the Golinsky Mine was inspected, and it was found that two of the mine portals had AMD flowing from them year round. This AMD flows into Little Backbone Creek and out into Shasta Lake. In the lake the AMD is diluted, but the heavy metal concentrations are a human health risk and have caused annual fish kills in Little Backbone Creek.

The Forest Service carried out an extensive site investigation of the Golinsky Mine in the '90s, and located all remaining features of the mining operations. Most existing remains are related to the second, short-lived gold recovery operation of the Vickery brothers in the 1930s. The only clearly identified remnants of the first phase, when the Golinsky's were running the mine, were found off to the side of the main mining operations. This appears to have been a fairly large building, perhaps a dormitory. Pottery and glass shards date it to the earlier Golinsky copper mining period. The search for the source of the AMD had a secondary purpose, which was to determine if there was any evidence to warrant the

Golinsky Mine site being declared a historic and/or cultural site. If that were the case, it would limit the options for dealing with the AMD, since any work at the portals could impact historical remains.

The mine site is as difficult to reach today as it ever was. The slope is very steep (70–100 percent). The soil and rock are prone to crumble and crash downhill. The upper reaches of the mine site are covered with dense, thorny vegetation (whitethorn, manzanita, and poison oak). In 1991 Daniel R. Elliot, a Forest Service archeologist, was sent to examine the site. He found extensive remains of the smelter sites, tram tracks, and mine adits, all dating from the second gold mining operations of the '20s and '30s.

Elliot's report went to other Forest Service personnel, and the conclusion was reached by them that this site had no cultural or architectural significance. It also stated that individuals associated with the Golinsky Mine "were not significant people in the local area. They did not develop or contribute any notable acts of commerce or community service." (*Archaeological Reconnaissance,* Faye P. Teach, 1991)

Indeed, it was necessary and desirable to eliminate the AMD flowing from the Golinsky Mine, but it seems outrageous, hasty, ignorant, and inaccurate to eliminate the Golinsky family from the history of the area. Most of the Golinsky's influence, as reported earlier, was felt in the town of Kennett. The creation of Shasta Lake wiped out the town of Kennett, and it seems to have done the same to the memory of the Mother and the Father of Kennett.

Because the site was not considered eligible to be added to the National Register of Historic Places, work to contain the AMD could proceed without impediment or delay. The Forest Service achieved its goal. Work went forward on the elimination of the AMD, using one of four proposed methods submitted by the U.S. Forest Service to the Environmental Protection Agency

(Tyrrel, 1991). The chosen plan consisted of building reinforced concrete bulkheads inserted into the three adits of the mine, keeping the polluted water in the mines. A heavy wire fence has been placed around the adits to keep people out of the dangerous tunnels. This project's work was completed in 2001.

Robert Tyrrel's report also mentioned evidence of disturbances to the site probably made during the 1970s or 1980s by persons unknown. Some of the leaching tanks had been dismantled; scattered lumber had been collected and stacked, possibly to be taken out at some future date. The area has few visitors, but hikers and adventurers make the climb several times a year. Locals consider it a challenging and interesting hike. Since there is no longer a town, it seems appropriate to acknowledge the Golinskys and the rich history left by them and other pioneer figures in the area by placing a historic marker at the trailhead to the mine or at some other appropriate spot.

The lure of gold and the romance of mines never seem to end. A Redding source has told me of many schemes to explore the Golinsky Mine, which rumor has it, still contains great riches. I have been shown a letter, written in May 1988, from Sidney Golinsky who claims to be "sole heir" of the family and the mine. He might be distantly related to Bernhard, who had a large number of siblings, most remaining in Europe. But Sidney never appeared during the lifetimes of Bernhard and Rosa. No such person is named in either of Rosa's or Bernhard's wills. He may be a sole survivor. The question is of what or whom?

The work by the EPA to close the entrances of the mine by installing a heavy fence should put an end to any attempts to explore the mine adits. These precautions may keep people out for the present, but it is doubtful that rumors of gold will cease.

The writing of the history of a place that has no remaining physical presence is a challenge. Kennett is not only gone, but it has been drowned. There are no abandoned buildings to explore, no streets to roam, no newspapers or books left lying around.

This means that any records kept by public officials are likely to be gone as well. I was told in 1988 by J. Paul Capener, project superintendent at Shasta Dam, that there had been as many as fifty cartons of records from Kennett stored in boxes in vaults at Shasta Dam. These boxes were scheduled to be transferred to the Shasta Historical Society, but they were lost in transit! Losing one or two cartons is somewhat credible, but losing fifty is more than careless. A possible explanation, believable to me at least, is that the records are still in some out-of-the-way vault-like room at Shasta Dam. On one visit to the dam in 1988 seeking material, I was shown into such a vault, deep inside of the dam. Walls, ceilings, and floors were concrete; the door was metal and the walls were lined with old, four-drawer olive green metal filing cabinets. The entire place was lit by only a single bulb hanging from the ceiling. No one at the dam could tell me the arrangement of the topics in the files, nor how I could get more light. I began to have visions of being locked in and my body never found again, so in haste I abandoned the search at that locale!

Another possible source of information about Kennett was contained in the three newspapers published at various times in Kennett. The California State Library has undertaken the project of making microfilm copies of all California newspapers. Unfortunately this was not done with the Kennett newspapers. Probably so few Kennett newspapers could be found at the time of the microfilming project that it was deemed worthless. Luckily, the Redding papers were microfilmed and the news I found there forms the backbone for much of this book. Redding, being the larger, earlier community, took up the task of reporting on activities in the rest of Shasta County including Kennett. The Redding *Free Press* began reporting on the area in 1883. The name of this paper has changed over the years and it exists today under the masthead *The Record Searchlight*. Anyone who has been obliged to get material from microfilm sources will understand that my eyes became seriously strained in my search for material on Kennett. A few single copies of Kennett papers can be found at the Shasta Historical Society in Redding and the California State Library in Sacramento. They are tantalizing and create an urge in me to start searches of the attics and basements of Redding area homes. I did advertise in the *Record Searchlight*, but with no helpful results.

Afterword

Although this book takes its title from a single small mining town in California, its story tells of experiences true in many other such communities. At certain times during the operations of mines in the Kennett area, it was indicated that ore was sent to the former ASARCO smelter near Tacoma, Washington. There is also a closed ASARCO smelter in Everett, Washington, north of Seattle. The soil around it is so contaminated that it is seventy-percent percent arsenic in some spots, according to an article in the *Seattle Post Intelligencer* (June 11, 2002). The Washington State Department of Ecology has ordered the company to excavate up to 25,000 cubic yards of the most polluted area at the former smelter site. This soil has arsenic concentrations of over 3,000 parts per million and is in a fenced and guarded area. The company has been ordered by the EPA to clean up more than 500 contaminated homes and businesses located downwind from the smelter. ASARCO is challenging its liability for damage caused a hundred years ago arguing that they were operating legally at that time.

ASARCO is also working on the cleanup of thirty toxic waste sites nationally, including the former smelter near Tacoma, Washington, which has tainted neighborhoods in the south King County area. Environmental groups have been urging reform of the 1872 General Mining law. The law currently allows mining companies to extract precious metals from public land without paying the government for the minerals, and to privatize public land containing gold, silver, and other metals by paying five dollars an acre or less—prices unchanged since President U. S. Grant signed the mining law in 1872 (*The Seattle Post Intelligencer,* January 25, 2002).

Mark Rey, undersecretary of agriculture, who oversees the U.S. Forest Service, speaking at a Northwest Mining Association meeting in Spokane, Washington, in December 2001, told the miners attending he would "reinvigorate" the unit that oversees mining on Forest Service land, which he said had languished during the Clinton presidency (*Post Intelligencer,* January 25, 2002).

The Golinsky Mine sits on Forest Service land above Shasta Lake, its adits plugged with cement bulkheads and encircled by a heavy-duty fence, out of action forever—or is it? Will it be "reinvigorated?" Will the plugged adits to the Golinsky Mine be dynamited or hammered out? Will gold seekers return? The Golinsky Mine has seemed to have had a life of its own. For good or for ill, will there be another chapter to its life?

The preceding questions had barely been asked and this book was being typeset when new news was released. The Bureau of Reclamation is studying a plan to add 6.5 to 18.5 feet of concrete to the top of Shasta Dam! This is one of several possibilities to increase the water supply for a growing population.

An 18.5-foot elevation would boost Shasta Lake by 15 percent and allow more water downstream. This proposal is part of the recently enacted federal water bill, Cal-Fed, chiefly authored by Senator Diane Feinstein. Feinstein is quoted in *The Sacaramento Bee* (November 22, 2004) saying, "I believe it is a God-given right as Californians to be able to water gardens and lawns."

Residents located above Shasta Dam feel they have a God-given right not to be flooded. Victims of an elevated dam include a family owning historic property on the McCloud River, present-day Wintu Indian villages and burial sites, and lakeside recreational businesses among others.

Steve Evans, director of Friends of the Sacramento River in Sacramento points out that raising the dam would violate a state law that protects the McCloud River from any more dams and reservoirs.

We can now pose new questions. Will Slaughter Island, the last hint of Kennett's existence, be drowned? Will rising water reach mine adits and cause acid mine drainage to flow into Shasta Lake? Is the structure of the Pit River Bridge endangered? What will happen to the railroad tracks and tunnels that were moved once to accomodate the present Lake Shasta? Are there viable alternatives to this plan?

The future around the area of Kennett is again threatened for those whose livelihood and lifestyle may be jeopardized by raising Shasta Dam. We must wait to see what develops.

References

Allen, Marion V. (ed.) 1987. *Shasta Dam and Its Builders.* Shingletown, CA.

Alzueta, C. (1967). "The bonanza days and decline of Kennett." *The Covered Wagon,* Shasta Historical Society, Redding. CA, 11–16.

Alzueta, C. (1989). "A Road for the Iron Horse." *Covered Wagon,* Shasta Historical Society, Redding. CA, 4–19.

Anonymous. (1905). "Kennett and Vicinity." *Free Press Annual,* Redding, CA.

Averill, C.V. (1939). "Mineral Resources of Shasta County." *California Journal of Mines and Geology, 35* (1), 108–191.

Bureau of Reclamation. (1992). *Golinsky Mine.* Sacramento, CA: Anon.

Bush, H. E. (1964). "In the Shadow of the Mountain: The New Era of Mining in Shasta County." *Covered Wagon,* Shasta Historical Society, Redding, CA. 37–38

Chapman, H. M. (1988). "My memories of Kennett and the Old Mammath Copper Mine." *Covered Wagon,* Shasta Historical Society, Redding, CA, 11–15.

Ditmar, H. O. F. (ed.). (1913), *Copper Outlook,* Kennett, CA.

Du Bois, C. (1935). *Wintu Ethnography*. Berkeley, CA: University of California Press.

Elliot, D. (1991). *A brief history of the Golinsky Mine.* Unpublished manuscript (mimeograph). Redding, CA.: U.S. Forest Service.

Frank, B. F., & Chappell, H. W. (1881). *The History and Business Directory of Shasta County*. Redding, CA: Redding Independent Book and Job Printing House.

Giles, R. (1949). *Shasta County, California.* Oakland, CA: Biobooks.

Grenfell, D. C. (1989). "One Summer in Kennett." *Covered Wagon*, Shasta Historical Society, Redding, CA, 78–81.

Guilford-Kardell, M. (1980). "Some Precontact Shasta Wintu Site Locations, Circa 1850." *Occasional papers of the Redding Museum*, Redding, CA, No. 1.

Heizer, R. F. (ed.) (1993). *The Destruction of California Indians.* Lincoln, NB.: University of Nebraska Press.

Heizer, R. F., & Elasser, A. B. (1980). *The Natural World of the California Indians*. Berkeley, CA: University of California Press.

Jones, W., A. (1985). "Prosperity vs. Pollution: The Shasta Copper Mining Controversy." *The Californians,* March/April 1995, 34–37.

Kinkel, A. R., Jr., Hall, W. E., and Albers, J. P. (1956). "Geology and Base-metal Deposits of West Shasta Copper-Zinc District, Shasta County, California." *Geological Survey Professional Paper No. 285.* Washington, D.C.: United States Government Printing Office.

Kristophers, K. V. (1973). *The Copper Mining Era in Shasta County, California, 1896–1919: An environmental impact study.* Unpublished master's thesis, California State University, Chico, CA.

Kroeber, A. L. (1976). *Handbook of the Indians of California*. New York: Dover Books. (Originally published as Bulletin #78 of Bureau of American Ethnology, Smithsonian Institution, 1925).

LaPena, F. B. (1978). "Wintu." *Handbook of North American Indians*, vol. 8. Washington, D.C.: Smithsonian Institution.

Limerick, P. N. (1987). *The Legacy of Conquest: The Unbroken Past of the American West.* New York: W. W. Norton and Company.

Lowden, S. E. (1977). "Life at the Mammoth Mine, 1907–1918." *The Covered Wagon.* Shasta Historical Society Redding, CA, 31–41.

McKim, H. (ed.). (1985). *A History of Shasta County, California.* Redding, CA: Shasta Historical Society.

Miller, J. (1996). *Life Amongst the Modoc: Unwritten History.* Berkeley, CA.: Heyday Books. (Originally published 1873.)

Montarbo, R. L. (1969). "Kennett, a Glance into a Lost City's Past." Unpublished manuscript. Redding, CA: Shasta College.

Peterson, C. (1970). "Kennett Beginning to End." Unpublished manuscript. California State University, Chico, CA.

Rocca, A. M. (1993). *The Shasta Dam Boomtowns.* Redding, CA: Redding Museum of Art and History.

Rocca, A. M. (1995). *America's Shasta Dam, a History of Construction 1936–1945.* Redding, CA: Redding Museum of Art and History.

Scanlon, H. F. (1968). "Through the Sacramento River Canyon in 1841." *The Siskiyou Pioneer,* vol. 4, no. 1, pp. 63–67. Yreka, CA.

Signor, J. B. (1982). *Rails in the Shadow of Mt. Shasta.* Burbank, CA: Howell-Norton Books.

Smith, D. (1991). *The Dictionary of Early Shasta County History.* Cottonwood, CA: Self-published.

Tillotson, W. D. "Redding Then and Now," *Covered Wagon,* Shasta Historical Society Redding, CA, 39–40.

Waldman, C. (1985). *Atlas of the North American Indians.* New York: Facts on File Publications.

Waldron, D. (1971). *Kennett Last Boom Town of Shasta County,* unpublished student research paper, California State University, Chico.

Wilhelmson, T. J. (1967). *The Town of Kennett and the Mammoth Mine*, unpublished student research paper, California State University, Chico.

Woodrum, H. C. (1987). Doctors on horseback, *Covered Wagon*, Shasta Historical Society, Redding CA, 68–75.

Women of the West Museum, (2003). *Women Suffrage.* Retrieved July 2, 2003, from http:www.autry-museum.org

World Almanac, (2003). *San Francisco Earthquake.* Retrieved July 2, 2003, from http.wwwinformationplease.com

Newspapers, Redding, California

Republican Free Press: 1883–1888

Free Weekly Press: 1888–1891

Free Press: April, 1888–March 1906

Courier-Free Press: March 1906–June 13, 1916; 1941–42

Redding Record: 1941–42

Other California Newspapers

The Searchlight: Relevant dates

Alta California: 1849–1865

Frank Leslie's Illustrated Newspaper: December 1855–1906

Copper Outlook: May 14, 1915, published in Kennett

San Francisco Chronicle: March 23, 2000

The Sacramento Bee: November 22, 2004

Other Newspapers

Seattle Post-Intelligencer, various dates

Seattle Times, various dates

Interviews (Personal Correspondence)

John Balma, June 1992.

Mr. and Mrs. (Margaret) Rudy Balma, June 1992.

Rhonda Bowers, environmental engineer, U. S. Forest Service, Redding, CA, various dates 1992–2003.

J. Paul Capener, project superintendent, Shasta Dam, May 1988.

G. H. Gibbs, retired professor of history, Shasta College, Redding, CA, 1996–1997.

Margaret Guilford-Kardell, Blaine, WA, numerous letters and conversations, 1989–2002.

Mrs. Georgia Hanson, 1995.

Hazel McKim, Shasta Historical Society, letters and telephone calls, 1985–2000.

Robert B. Tyrrel. 1990–1991, forest supervisor, U.S. Forest Service, Redding, CA.

Family Informants

Rubie Radzinski Blumenthal

Jay Corson and Marjorie Cohen Geballe (grandchildren of Hennie Golinsky Gans)

Ronald Geballe

Cindy Gilman Redburn and John Gilman (grandchildren of Jake [Golinsky] Gilman)

Jane Portis Kaplan, 2001–2002

Index

A

B

C

D

E

F

G

H

L

M

N

O

P

R

S

T

U

V

W

Y

About the Author

Jane Schuldberg

Jane Schuldberg was born and raised in the Chicago area. She is a graduate of the University of Chicago. She worked as a story analyst at Warner Bros. She and her physician husband moved to Seattle. There she was active in the League of Women Voters.

Schuldberg founded the Snow Goose, a Seattle gallery devoted to authentic Eskimo and Northwest Coast Indian art. She traveled extensively in the Arctic meeting native artists while seeking artwork for her gallery. She has two children and resides in Chico, California, near her daughter and family.